TIBET AND NEPAL

TIBET AND NEPAL

PAINTED & DESCRIBED

A. H. SAVAGE LANDOR

GYAN

Published by

GYAN

Gyan Publishing House
5, Ansari Road
Daryaganj, New Delhi-110002
Phone: 011-47034999, 9811692060
E-mail: books@gyanbooks.com

Distribution Network
gyanbooks.com
India, USA, Canada, UK, Australia, France

ISBN : 978-81-212-4109-0 (PB)
First Published, London, 1905

2nd Impression 2020

Printed at: Gyan Press, Delhi.

TIBET & NEPAL

PAINTED & DESCRIBED BY

A. HENRY SAVAGE LANDOR

PUBLISHED BY A. & C. BLACK
SOHO SQUARE · LONDON · W

Published January 1905

LIST OF ILLUSTRATIONS

CHAPTER I

"ONCE you have visited the snows of the Himahlyas," said a venerable old man of Kumaon to me, "you will have to return to them time after time until you die. When away from them, all through your life you will ever see them before you in your dreams."

Well, that was quite so; and that is what everybody feels who has spent some time on the higher elevations of that majestic range of mountains. To any one who appreciates Nature in all its grandeur, the fascination is so great that everything else in the way of scenery sinks into perfect insignificance by their side.

It is, to my mind, rather a pity that in England people have not yet learnt to call that range by its proper and poetic name "Himahlyas," by which the range is known all over Asia, instead of the distorted "Himalayas," which has no meaning whatever except to natives of these foggy little islands. The Americans, I am glad to say, when the corrected pronunciation was pointed out, at once accepted it, and it is now taught in all the schools.

Two years had elapsed since my first journey across Tibet, and I was still suffering greatly from the effects of the tortures and wounds which had been inflicted upon me during my captivity in the Forbidden Land. Nor did banquets and receptions and interviewers, autograph-collectors, etc., much help to rebuild my constitution. In fact, while in London, instead of improving I was getting weaker and more of an invalid every day.

In doctors I have no superabundant faith, but somehow or other felt that a little change from the monotony of a civilised existence, in the shape of chasing about their country some of my Tibetan friends who had tortured me, might possibly be of some benefit to my health. And if you take it into your head that something will do you good, it is not unusual that some sort of a cure results from it.

So, again I bundled my blankets, my surveying instruments, several cameras, and hundreds of plates, provisions, and painting materials, and by the first P. and O. steamer sailed for Bombay. From that place I went by rail to Kathgodam, thence by trail to the hill-station Almora in the North-West Provinces, which I again made my starting-point, as in the first journey.

Perhaps it may interest the reader to know that the entire preparations, the selection of all my followers, the purchase of an excellent Tibetan pony, and of all the outfit and provisions to last my men several months, were accomplished in the short space of twelve hours.

The selection of men for the type of expeditions I undertake, in which abnormal endurance is required, is not an easy matter, but I was particularly fortunate on that occasion. Big athletic fellows I generally avoid as absolutely useless for work requiring steady endurance and quick perception. I gave preference to small, determined, wiry men, light in weight, supple and quick in their movements.

Having satisfied myself that they were perfectly sound in lungs, heart, and digestive organs—they were, indeed, too sound in the latter respect—we were ready to start the following day. Each man carried a weight of 20 seers (or 40 lbs.), a light load, as I intended doing double and treble marches daily.

It was my intention to do a considerable amount of mountaineering *en route*, and I did it; but, contrary to the usual custom of British mountaineering expeditions (which set out with much flourish of trumpets) I did not burden myself with the company of Swiss Alpine guides. Here is the reason. I am well aware that it impresses a good many brainless folks to hear that an expedition to the Andes or the Himahlyas is accompanied, even led, by Swiss guides; but to any real mountaineer (I do not mean members of Alpine Clubs) the very fact that the members of such an expedition require guides at all is but a plain avowal that they have no faith in themselves, besides displaying a most infantile ignorance of how to find their way about. No mountaineer, who is a real mountaineer, ever needs to be told which is the best way to go up a mountain which is before him. His very instinct and observation tell him.

Let me remind you that the characteristics of mountains in different parts of the world vary to a considerable extent. It therefore seems to me that to employ a man (however fine a fellow he may be) who has spent his life hauling hysterical Alpinists by a much-beaten trail up Mont Blanc or the Matterhorn, to show the way up a virgin Himahlyan peak, is as delightfully absurd as it would be to charter an untravelled London cabman to show you with intelligence the sights of Moscow, or Bagdad, or Jerusalem! Do not forget, too, that Mont Blanc or the Matterhorn are perfectly insignificant hills when compared to peaks in the Himahlyas.

As you know, the chief hobby and boast of certain Alpinists is to climb mountains by impracticable ways. This practice is to be condemned. In plain words, any man who tries to go up a mountain by any but the easiest way is an idiot, and should be confined to a lunatic asylum. When difficulties arise, and many do, naturally they have to be overcome as best one can. Then again, there are many feats in mountaineering and rock-climbing which appear very dangerous and are not dangerous at all to any one with steady head, heart, and legs; but the absurd mania of obtaining notoriety by going up a peak by a dangerous route when an easier way exists has no more sense in it than were a horseman to try and ride his horse under its tail instead of upon its back! It is not real sport, and sport, above all things, should never be purposeless nor foolish.

Mountaineering, by any one in full possession of all his senses, is a delightful amusement, and possibly the pleasantest, healthiest, and most instructive exercise in existence. It develops every muscle in one's body, makes one quick of sight and hearing, expands, cleans, and purifies one's lungs, and it makes one—when dependent on oneself—a quick observer and a subtle student of Nature, its forces, and the ways of elements and how to counterbalance them. It should, therefore, be encouraged in any one born for the work; but, on the other hand, should be left severely alone by any one not specially constructed for the work by Mother Nature. It can but mean disaster in the end, and it generally does.

Unfortunate, too, is the man who in "exploring mountaineering" follows the rules and regulations laid down by theoretical but inexperienced amateurs of certain Alpine institutions. A practical mountaineer has nothing to learn from such misleading publications, whether brought out under the patronage of Clubs or by some enterprising charlatan or other. The constant suggestions to provide oneself with all sorts of expensive and cumbersome tools, axes, alpenstocks, and other impedimenta are merely to swell the pockets of advertisers who support those publications, rather than to safeguard the life of intending mountaineers.

Personally, and I am speaking from a somewhat extensive experience, I owe my success and the lack of serious accidents in any of my mountaineering expeditions absolutely to the using none of the appliances recommended by Alpine clubs. I mention this at the outset to prevent the usual criticisms accusing me of having neglected precautions. It was done wilfully on my part, because, as far as mountaineering is concerned, I prefer to use what little common-sense I possess in preference to accepting the large amount of nonsense offered by other people.

I had spared no expense and trouble to obtain the best scientific instruments possible for taking observations, and they were specially manufactured for me, light in weight and extra strong, and with special cases to protect them from injury in the roughest of travelling. My instruments were tested at the Kew Observatory—both before going out of and after my return to England—and found in perfect condition.

All altitudes of importance were invariably measured with the hypsometrical apparatus, several boiling-point thermometers being successively used in the observation. For differential heights of no great significance aneroids were used. All bearings were taken with a prismatic compass, and for latitude and longitude a 6-inch sextant was used, a chronometer watch, mercury and plate-glass artificial horizons.

Necessarily, I carried maximum and minimum thermometers and all necessary instruments and appliances for surveying work, photography, painting, etc. Several rifles and double-barrelled guns, a revolver, eight thousand rounds of ammunition, and ten pounds of gunpowder were carried, in case we had to do some shooting; while each man was given a large Gurkha *kukri* for his own protection.

For our needs I carried money in solid silver and gold. My tinned provisions were prepared for me in London, and were very good. All my most valuable possessions were packed in air-tight cases of my own design, which, as on previous journeys, I found answered very well.

A Tibetan tent, 7 feet high, 10 feet long, and

8 feet wide, twelve pounds only in weight; a small *tente d'abri,* and some shelters formed my camp.

Last, but not least, let me give some advice regarding your clothing when you go mountaineering. Do not masquerade for the occasion in fancy tweeds of startling cut, clumsy mufflers and gloves, and patent hobnailed boots. Wear the sort of clothes and footgear you are accustomed to put on every day. You will feel a great deal more comfortable, less ridiculous, and certainly a great deal safer.

Personally, I wear the same sort of clothing—serge suits of the thinnest tropical material—in any country and in any climate, with no underwear; thin socks, shoes of medium weight with no nails under the soles. I am very fortunate in one way, never feeling the slightest inconvenience through intense heat or cold. It is partly due, I think, to one's constitution and circulation of one's blood, partly to habit, and a good deal to being hardened through constant roughing.

Perhaps others, with not so rough a training, may not go quite so far; but never forget that the more you feel at your ease in your attire, the less you are hampered with articles of any kind which you are not accustomed to use every day, the more successful you will be in your mountaineering expeditions—especially on unknown mountains.

CHAPTER II

FROM Almora to the Tibetan frontier I followed, to a great extent, a different route from the one I had taken on my first journey, as I wanted to visit *en route* the interesting shrine of Debi Dhura. The character of the country traversed varied little from that already described in a previous work. I will only in this book describe things and places and incidents of the journey that are quite new, leaving out a detailed account of my itinerary.

Passing through forests of walnut trees, fine oak and deodars, *kaiphal*, rhododendrons, *utis*, and yew, and travelling at elevations varying from 5510 feet at Almora to 6630 feet at Debi Dhura, I reached in two days' journey the sacred temple situated on a great granitic plateau, the ridge of which extends for several miles.

It was in the afternoon. During the entire journey rain had come down in torrents; but as I arrived at Debi Dhura, the storm, which had been particularly fierce that day, cleared as by magic; the heavy, leaden-black clouds rolled away on every side, leaving behind most exquisite tints, of gold and red and green, of a superb sunset. With the wind rising, the white mist which covered the valleys below us rose slowly like a curtain, and a magnificent panorama shone in radiant beauty in the now crystalline atmosphere. Beyond the lower and nearer ranges of pure cobalt blue and dark warm greens, towered to the north snow-clad mountains of absolutely sublime beauty.

Shortly after my arrival an old priest came to greet me. He had in his hands a brass vessel filled with red flowers which he offered me, begging me to follow him to the shrine across the road.

"This is the world-famous shrine of Debi Dhura, the shrine to Mahadeva Varahi Debi and Bhimden," said he, with a series of grand salaams. "Ah, sahib, your health and soul will greatly benefit by your visit here," muttered the cunning old rascal, who by now had been joined by other priests.

We walked up past the sacred swings to the temple standing on the crown of a hill among really beautiful deodar, walnut, oak, and *Olea fragrans* trees. The temple itself was of no interest or beauty, but curious indeed were the gigantic boulders leaning against each other, allowing a narrow entrance into a cave containing a well and a shrine.

No foreigner is allowed inside the cave, for it is —they say—the home of Debi, and must not be desecrated by humans of other faiths. My men seemed greatly excited over their visit to the cave, and they were profound in their salaams. They were muttering fervent prayers when they came out. On being asked what they had seen inside, they would not or could not say. As a matter of fact, I believe they had seen nothing, for the cave was very dark.

On we went, down some slippery steps, until we came—some hundred yards below—to a curious rock rising to a great height above the ground.

"Ransila, the giant," called out the priest, pointing at the rock and calling it by its name.

We climbed upon it to examine the extraordinary crack which split the rock in two. The fissure was so clean and sharp that it seemed produced by a violent blow rather than by the action of water. A similar crack was noticeable in a lower rock, and neither of these fissures seemed very ancient. Lightning may have caused them, or more possibly an earthquake.

The explanation given by the priests was quaint, and it was interesting to watch the expressions on my men's faces, who received with great suspicion my matter-of-fact explanation of how those cracks came to be; whereas they gazed open-mouthed and took in unreservedly the fairy legend recited to us by the priest. Here is the legend.

Bhim Sen or Bem Sing and Debi were one day playing *pachisi*, a game resembling chess, and very common in India. They were seated on the above-described granitic boulder, "the Ransila," and to give colour to this narrative a square engraved in the rock marks the spot where they sat. Other mystic signs, marks, and figures are also pointed out to credulous pilgrims. It appears that while so engaged, Bem Sing heard the voice of a *shert*, a rich man, drowning in the distant ocean, hundreds and hundreds of miles away. He listened. The *shert* prayed God to live.

Regardless of the fact that the distance from Debi Dhura to the ocean is, as the crow flies, at least 700 miles, Debi remained quite unconcerned, and continued to play the game with his right hand, while he stretched—the legend does not say whether to its full extent—the left arm and lifted from the foaming water not only the drowning man but the sinking ship as well.

On withdrawing his arm and resting it upon his lap the attention of his partner as well as of the onlookers was attracted by the wet on Debi's hand and forearm. They inquired the cause, but Debi curtly requested them to mind their own business and go on with the game. Puzzled and angry, the others demanded an explanation. Insulting remarks were made and, finding no other explanation, a suggestion was made that he was perspiring something else instead of perspiration from his arm. At this point Debi deemed it prudent to vanish.

Bem Sing's wrath was at its zenith. Amazed, even upset, he searched for Debi all around, and, unable to find him, he seized a large boulder and with it struck the big rock Ransila with such violence that he split it in two, in order to discover whether Debi was hiding inside it.

The onlookers in the meantime, terrified by the doings of these abnormal beings, had fled in all directions, while Debi had quietly retired to the cave which I have already described, and where—they say—he dwells still. The boulder used by Bem Sing in his feat of strength is shown to this day to the open-mouthed pilgrims at Debi Dhura. So firmly had he grasped it in his hands that the marks of his fingers and thumbs are still deeply impressed upon the granite.

The end of the legend brought forth the usual request for a generous backshish, while more flowers were produced and handed to my followers, who adorned their ears and caps with them.

We returned to the sacred swings, of great height, with iron chains instead of ropes, upon which pilgrims, old and young, swing themselves, either singly or in couples. During the months of June, July, and August, when a pilgrimage and fair are held at the shrine, these swings are kept going all day and the greater part of the night. Thousands upon thousands of devotees visit the weird rocks and leave handsome oblations. A special festival is held in August, when throngs of natives assemble and sacrifice goats, sheep, and occasionally buffaloes. As many as one hundred sheep are killed during one of these festivals, and the sacrifice takes place either on the Ransila rock or at the entrance of the cave.

THE SACRED SWINGS OF DEBI DHURA

The "stone of luck" is to be noticed beyond the first swing.

Everything at Debi Dhura is connected with stones and rocks. Between the two swings and near a quadrangular stone wall some four or five feet high, lay a big natural ball of granite, called "Chela," or "the test of strength." They say that only one man in a hundred can raise it above the ground, one in a thousand is able to lift it up to his waist, and not a human being alive can lift it up and deposit it on the wall. Whoever performed the latter deed would have every happiness for ever. Although according to the priests the stone weighed 4000 lbs., its actual weight was not more than 350 lbs.; only it was difficult to get hold of it, and it was well-nigh impossible to do so by sheer strength. But when brute strength fails, ruse is often easily successful, and so, being somewhat versed in the laws of leverage, balance, and impetus, I succeeded, much to the amazement of everybody, in placing that stone upon the wall. It was an effort though, I can tell you.

A peculiar feature of the annual fair is the procession from the shrine in the cave to the summit of the hill, a few hundred yards off, upon which is a stone shed and a cairn. The men who carry the stone idol in this procession are all stark-naked,—a very unusual case with Hindoos,

—and so also are many who follow in the procession.

Another feature of the festival is that strange custom which one finds in most countries of Asia—the annual stone-fights. About a thousand men collect in an open space, and are divided into legions of five hundred each, a short distance from each other. When both parties have amassed in their respective camps a suitable amount of ammunition in the way of stones, collected in mounds, and also a good supply carried on the person, the combatants draw nearer and nearer in a line. At a signal the fight begins, and they fling stones at one another by means of slings and forked sticks, whirling the missiles through the air with terrific force. The more people get injured the fiercer becomes the fight, till the ammunition fails,—and it lasts a long time, because the combat is, as it were, a mere exchange of ammunition.

The wives and daughters and sweethearts of the combatants view the *melée* with trembling hearts from a raised point of vantage well out of range of the missiles. The fighters get to such close quarters that pounding one another on the head with stones is not uncommon, and it is only when all are worn, wounded, aching, and blinded by the dust and blood that an armistice is called. Hardly any one escapes unhurt, but no one ever complains, no matter how serious their wounds may be, as they believe that no one can actually be killed in these sacred fights. As each man falls senseless to the ground, he is conveyed to the temple where the following treatment awaits him. The Brahmin priests beat and rub him well with a bunch of nettles. It is said to be an infallible remedy.

No ill-feeling is said to remain between the legions after the fight is over, and with bandaged heads and limbs they all join in a common *bura kana*—a big meal.

The fights generally begin by the children being made to fight first, the elders joining in when well excited over their sons' doings.

CHAPTER III

The trail, which had made a somewhat circuitous deviation southward of Debi Dhura, began to turn to the east, and soon after towards the north-east. After leaving Debi Dhura it brought the traveller to the summit of the granitic range which the trail followed all along, amidst country thickly wooded with oaks, rhododendrons, pines, and deodars. The whole journey was made at high elevations, through dense forests, with a feeling of damp about everything; the trees, soaked and dripping, standing like black giants in the penetrating white mist that enveloped us. One could not see more than twenty or thirty yards off.

In many places the trail was narrow, and it had been built by blasting the steep rocky mountain-side and filling whatever gaps there were with a wall supported on outstanding boulders below.

The trail was in such places hardly more than three or four feet wide, and no parapet of any kind existed to prevent unlucky travellers from falling over into the precipice several hundred feet in depth at the side.

In fair weather, when the trail was dry, and when a trustworthy animal was being ridden, there would, of course, be no danger of any kind; but when I went through, the path was slimy and slippery, and my pony—although excellent and sure-footed, quite like a goat on a mountain trail—possessed the bad habit of shying at anything moving upon the ground, and particularly at the whitewashed milestones, when he would invariably make a few contortions, and end up by standing on his hind legs with a final leap forward when the whip was duly applied upon his back.

I had just passed one of these mile-posts, and expecting a peaceful ride until we came to the next, I pulled out my notebook and was jotting down some observations. We were then at a considerable height, the trail, cut into the rock, winding its way along the summit of the mountain-side. It was about sunset, and everything around me was silent but for the clatter of my pony's hoofs upon the wet trail, or every now and then the noise of a stone rolling down into the precipice some 800 feet deep.

In going round a corner a man appeared enveloped in a red blanket, the end of which was fluttering in the breeze. Unexpectedly my pony neighed frantically, gave a powerful jerk, backed, and slipped with his hind legs off the trail.

"Jupiter!" I exclaimed as I tried to jump off the saddle. My blood turned cold; but before I had time to dismount, the pony which was resting with his body on the trail, scrambled up again on it in the most miraculous manner. In a perfect frenzy he now bolted full gallop along the tortuous and narrow way. In my attempt to get off, the reins had got loose and entangled, and I had taken my left foot off the stirrup.

A glance at the illustration depicting this incident will show the kind of place where it occurred; and it can easily be imagined that a pony, dashing along round corners involved some minor dangers to the rider, such as smashing one's knee or head against projecting boulders. Worse luck, in this unpleasant contingency, the bit broke, which placed me absolutely at the mercy of the pony, who viciously rubbed against the rocks to my right, so that the right stirrup and part of the saddle were

AN AWKWARD MOMENT

torn off. My right leg might have shared the same fate had nature not endowed me with sufficient agility to move it out of the way when necessary. Dismounting would have meant certain death, because, at the speed I was going, no matter on which side I got off, either directly or by recoil, I should have been shot off into the abyss.

Eventually—and when it pleased him—the pony resumed the journey in a less reckless fashion. If not the best-tempered, he was certainly the most sure-footed animal I had ever ridden, and eventually he and I became good friends; he lost his shyness and never again played tricks. He was really as good as a goat at hill-climbing, and he could go where a human would experience difficulty in getting along.

Two of my men, who, with trembling hearts, had witnessed the accident, ultimately caught me up and explained to me the real cause of it. Simultaneously with the appearance of the man in the flapping blanket, the pony had placed his foot on a small snake lying coiled and numbed with cold upon the road.

We had double and treble marches daily, drenching rain, and heavy trails, but pony and men went well. The pony, I must say, lost a good deal of his friskiness, for, in order to remove his exuberance of vigour as quickly as possible, I permitted some of my men to indulge in their national habit of holding to the pony's tail while ascending steep hills.

We seemed to have a good many varied experiences on that trip; the next sight being the corpse of a woman tied in a sheet to a pole, and sprinkled all over with red paint. A group of men sat by her, and seemed concerned at the unwelcome appearance of a *sahib*.

The woman had been lynched. She was said to have been beautiful, but unfaithful to her husband, for which latter fault she had been dragged into the forest, ill-treated, and eventually hanged, her body being left for several days until the murder was discovered. On the present occasion the body was being conveyed to Almora—some fifty miles off—for the official examination and inquiry. I had dismounted in order to hear the details of the tragedy, but as the corpse was in a state of decomposition I jumped on the saddle again and fled, my handkerchief held fast to my nose.

I was told that Kumaonis, especially in the particular part of the province I was then travelling in, were very revengeful and much addicted to murder. I, too, found them morose and sulky, ever discontented, somewhat quick-tempered and unreasonable. They undoubtedly possess the vindictive and warlike characteristics of their former masters and present neighbours, the Nepalese, but have lost—or possibly never possessed—any of their finer qualities.

Since the British took possession of this part of Kumaon, crime has been put down to a certain extent, but much difficulty, I understand, is experienced in ever discovering offenders, who are cleverly screened from the authorities by everybody. They certainly have no love, nor even respect, for *sahibs*, and they display a supercilious look upon their countenances which makes them heartily detestable.

I was able to obtain additional ponies and men at Lohagart, formerly a military cantonment, and to continue my journey towards the Nepalese frontier.

We crossed the Serju River forming the southern and northern boundaries, respectively, between the Sor and Kali Kumaon Parganahs, by a forced march of twenty-one miles—quite good going with baggage and on such roads in such weather. We had some difficulty in keeping to the trail in the dark forest at night, and we had a curious instance of how superstition will work on some people's minds with quite disastrous effects. All over the Himahlyas one finds, in some form or other, a rooted belief in the spirits of the mountains and of the forest, some of the spirits being benign enough, others of a wicked temperament.

My *sayce*, who was an excellent fellow, but timid to a degree, had become separated from the rest of my party and had remained far behind in charge of a recalcitrant pony and load. In the middle of the night I heard distant cries of distress, and, suspecting the cause, I sent some men with improvised torches to his assistance. They carried in the *sayce*, and on depositing him on the ground, pronounced him dying. In fact, the poor fellow was doubled up, delirious with fever, and in a state of absolute nervous collapse. When I brought a light to his face he became terrified, wept, and, trembling all over, begged for mercy. He seemed to be labouring under some hallucination—some ghastly vision at all events, for when I placed my hand upon his forehead he screamed and struggled in horror. He entreated to be freed from the horrible figures which danced around him; he shuddered, and eventually his convulsions took the form of an epileptic fit.

This was all the result of a prolonged fright. When he recovered sufficiently he told me how at night in the forest, when he was left alone, evil spirits surrounded him and pulled him by the hair, the ears, the nose, and pinched him all over.

"Show me the marks."

"*Sahib*," he said, looking at himself all over, "I can see no marks, but I still feel the pain where they touched me."

"But how could you see the spirits if it was quite dark?"

"Yes, but it seemed to grow quite light when they suddenly appeared. I think they were the souls of dead people. They were very ugly, *sahib!*"

"Were they as ugly as we are?"

"Yes, *sahib*, about the same! I think I recognised some of my relations among them."

The poor fellow's nerves were so shattered by the fright he had experienced that he never completely recovered from the shock.

In other works I have described how the natives on the borders of Tibet fear these spirits of the mountains, and place obstacles, such as thorns, etc., along the paths in order to prevent them entering villages, while threads are placed along dangerous passages upon trails to facilitate the "good spirits of the mountains" of departed friends finding their way in the dark of the night without misadventure.

Going now in a northerly direction we came to Pithoragarh, a place of former importance, possessing the remains of a Nepalese fort, an elaborate structure of solid earth-works with platform for guns, a water-tank, and a much-loopholed quadrangular castle. These structures stand on prominent points in the centre of the green and well-cultivated valley,—some fourteen square miles in extent,—dotted here and there with little villages and houses and tufts of trees, and irrigated by several streams. A low hill-range in the centre separates the valley in two.

While taking a photograph of the forts I nearly and most unexpectedly trod on a big snake, some 8 feet in length, which lay spread in the sun. He raised his prettily arched neck at my approach and hissed with some vehemence, which I took for a request to stand back. Motionless, he gazed at me with his vitrine eyes, and he was so beautiful, with iridescent scales shining like precious stones in the sun, that for one moment I could not help gazing at him. But as I had no stick nor any weapon upon me I cut short my part of this mutual admiration. When the snake described a graceful curve and departed, I, too, with somewhat less grace, made a speedy retreat in the opposite direction.

From Pithoragarh by quick marches I made rapid progress towards the frontier, visiting *en route* my old friend the Rajiwar of Askote, who had shown me much kindness when conveyed over the frontier after my captivity and tortures in Tibet two years previously. The entire town turned out to receive me, and I was again entertained by the Rajah in his palace.

It seemed rather a pity that this magnificent old fellow, whose faithfulness to the British had ever been exemplary, did not receive more courtesy from snobbish officials who occasionally visited his country, because, after all, courtesy costs nothing and goes a very long way with natives of all classes. The important services which he and his family have rendered in frontier matters with both Tibet and Nepal seemed to have been forgotten, and with the heavy taxation that had been imposed upon him he found it difficult—at the time of my visit—to support himself and his numerous relations.

From a strategic point of view the Askote valley is the principal and practically the only highway, the key, as it were, to all the Himahlyan passes leading into Tibet from Bhot (both in Darma and in Bias), as well as those of Western Nepal. Perhaps the fact of having in such a spot a loyal subject, able to keep a sharp watch upon dangers that may impend in the future, would be more valued if it were more understood.

After a day of festivities and excessive eating, enlivened by most harmonious native music, and a visit from my friends the Raots, the proud wild men of the forest who had on a former occasion predicted my death when I visited their haunt, we travelled through the low and hot Kali valley. Here malarial fever was rampant, vermin and mosquitoes in swarms, and rinderpest raging. I was now going along the Nepalese frontier, the Kali River defining the boundary-line between the North-West Provinces of India and Nepal.

On entering Bhot, or Little Tibet, we again rose to greater altitudes, and were soon able to shake off the touch of fever which nearly all my men and

A DARAMSALLA

Type of mountain shelters in the Himahlyas, N.W. Nepal. On the highway to Tibet.

myself had contracted in going through the steamy, damp valley. At Sirka, since my former visit, a Christian church of stone had risen—the first one in British Tibet—the work of the untiring and self-sacrificing Miss Sheldon, an American lady doctor, who has for years done noble work among the Shokas,—Shoka, as you know, is the local name of the inhabitants of that particular section of Bhot. When I passed through, Miss Sheldon was busy putting on the roof of the church—an operation which I watched with admiration, mingled somewhat with concern, although I must confess a skilled mason could not have done it better.

CHAPTER IV

SOME miles farther on another surprise awaited me. A new trail was being cut along the rock to shorten the ups and downs of the old "Nerpani"—the "waterless trail"—or, rather, some of the worst parts of the old trail were being modified and straightened. The new trail was just as narrow and dangerous as the old one, in some places only a couple of feet or so wide, or even less, with a deep precipice beneath, and many parts, as with the older trail, were supported on crow-bars thrust into the rock, some slabs of stone placed upon them making the path.

But one thing the new trail certainly did. It did away with some of the interminable flights of steps which were one of the most trying features of the old Nerpani. So that both the Government and the Shokas who subscribed most of the money for the work, may be congratulated on the decided improvement of that highway into Tibet.

In former days it was almost impossible to take pack-animals across, except sheep,—and many of these always perished on each journey,—but by the new trail, when finished, this is feasible, although not easy.

For certain reasons of my own, and knowing the difficulty of obtaining ponies in Tibet itself, I decided to bring my pony across at all costs. It was certainly a job which gave me a great many hours of hard work and anxiety. The trail, blasted into the rock or in narrow flights of steps along the high cliffs, was wet and slippery, and in many places hardly broad enough for the animal's body to pass without losing its balance. Still, with a sling or two, and one man holding the beast by the head and another by the tail, we managed, with occasional precipitous slides, to get along pretty well. In one place the pony slipped and fell sideways on the wet slabs, and kicked fragments of the unsteady road (in that portion laid on crowbars) flying into the river, down, down below, some 600 or 700 feet sheer drop. In other places, where rough scaffolding, supported on ropes, had been erected along the vertical rock in order to cut holes for the crowbars, the work of conveying the pony across was by no means easy. The scaffolding was generally made of a couple of trees tied together horizontally and an occasional plank.

Perhaps the illustration representing one of these passages may give a better idea of the situation than a long description. It was impossible for the pony to walk on the scaffolding, so that we had to push him over and convey him across, suspended, as far as where the trail began again. This we did by means of several rope slings round his body. Then one man held the pony's head, while I held him by the tail—being the easiest to let go in case of misadventure.

As the weight of a pony is considerable, the men wound the ropes several times round their wrists; and at one moment, when we were all in the centre of the scaffolding, it creaked so, and a plank on which a man stood showed such elasticity when a good deal of the weight was centered on it, that I really thought we should all be precipitated down into the stream. As luck would have it—and we did sweat over the undertaking, although the day was intensely cold—we got safely on the other side.

Perhaps I may mention that never in my experience have I seen an animal more terrified than that

A MOMENT OF SUSPENSE

pony was on that occasion. When we stood him again upon *terra firma* his legs quivered so that it was quite painful to witness, and he neighed and neighed convulsively, and made the sound echo all down the valley. I may also add that from that same scaffolding, that same morning, one of the workmen had fallen over, and his body was dashed into an unrecognisable mass on some rocks in the foaming stream below.

I had heard most peculiar rumours from the natives that the Tibetans had come in great force on to British territory at Garbyang, and with great pomp and much beating of drums were proclaiming that the British Government were afraid of coming to Tibet, and that the entire Bias and Chaudas had now been ceded to Tibet.

It may be remembered that as early as 1898, after the return from my first journey to Tibet, I pointed out to the Government the abuses of Tibetan officials who came over to our side of the frontier, claimed *Sah-tal* or Land Revenue from British subjects, and even tortured unprotected natives on our side of the frontier if they refused to pay. Some prominence was given in the House of Commons to questions on this subject, and the Governor of the North-West

Provinces had to acknowledge that such was the case, but declared that steps would be taken to stop the abuses. That the *Sah-tal* was paid was admitted, but it was stated to be a trade tax, which was untrue, and possibly uttered in ignorance of facts. It was agreed that the payment of the *Sah-tal* by British subjects should, nevertheless, be stopped, and it was actually suspended.

Apart from the fact that the words *Sah-tal* in themselves mean "land revenue," and that it is paid on the amount of land possessed by Shokas on British soil, a further proof that it is a land tax is provided by the case of Darma Shokas, who pay the *Sah-tal* on their land to the Jong Pen of Taklakot, and who do no trading with that particular part of Tibet.

Furthermore, the Jong Pen of Taklakot receives the amount with the distinct understanding that it is a land tax, and not a trade tax, and as such it appears in Government reports by the few British officials who had been to the frontier, such as Mr. Sturt, Mr. Larkin, and other deputy commissioners and collectors, and the Political Agent on the spot. In Darma the *Sah-tal* was collected direct by Jong Pen's emissaries, but in Bias and Chaudas the Political Agent was made to act as a servant to the Tibetans, and after collecting the revenue handed it over to the Jong Pen's officials at Gungi and at Garbyang, two villages conveniently situated for the purpose.

Chaudas, being the most distant from the Tibet border, only paid a nominal sum of 11 rupees in cash, and some 14 rolls of rough cloth; but Garbyang, for instance (besides a real trade tax jointly with Chaudas of 370 boxes of grain, each containing some 24 lbs., and 14 boxes of coarse cloth), paid for *Sah-tal* the following items:—

	86 (three anna bits).
Oats	1230 lbs.
Saluk (right of pasture) .	2 Tibetan rupees.
Ghur (sweet paste) . .	4 balls.
Coarse cloth . . .	3 entire rolls.
Shoka liquor . . .	55 jars.
Timber	30 huge logs.
Iron	4 lbs.

Cakes, *sattoo*, charcoal, and liquor for collecting party.

The village of Kuti also paid a heavy *Sah-tal*.

Rupees	17
Oats	1210 lbs.
Saluk	2 rupees.
Garah cloth . . .	40 yards.
Haunches of mutton . .	12
Jars of *chökti* (wine) . .	50
Ghur	28 balls.
Iron	2 lbs.

and charcoal, cakes, meat, liquor, etc.

Darma paid some 150 balls of *ghur*, which had a local value of about 75 rupees.

Notwithstanding that the Government of the North-West Provinces could not or would not see matters in the right light, it was a great gratification to me to think that, on my giving publicity to such an injustice, the Government had at last deemed it right to discontinue the payment of the land revenue to Tibetans by our frontier subjects. It came, therefore, as a very great surprise to me, on approaching Garbyang, to hear that the Tibetans had come over to that place in great force,—with the sanction of the British Government,—and that several officials, including a Nerba, some Dhats in red and black tunics and long swords, four *jimidars*, two drummers, and a number of soldiers were parading the streets, proclaiming the annexation of the district to Tibet, and ill-using the natives who differed. They were gorging themselves at the expense of the natives, and having a fine time all round.

At the request of a deputation of Shokas, I hastened on to Garbyang; but the Tibetans, believing that I was coming up with a large and well-armed expedition to take a revenge upon them for former misdeeds, deemed it advisable to pack up their chattels, pocket their pride, and decamp over the frontier.

I met with a most enthusiastic reception from the Garbyalis, who wished me to remain in their village until the passes were closed up by snow so as to keep their compulsory guests away. The Shokas seemed depressed and disgusted at what they rightly believed unwarrantable treachery on the part of the Government of India. They had always been faithful—even under trying circumstances—to the British, and such undeserved treatment led them to the one conclusion, preached by full-powered Tibetan lungs, that England must indeed be weak, or at least afraid of Tibet.

Undoubtedly these sad and unchecked occurrences all along our Tibetan frontier—you see, it is so uncomfortable for Anglo-Indian officials to go up to the snows to make inquiries and so on—have been the chief cause of Tibetan aggressiveness. There is no man so brave as the one who believes his opponent is not going to fight; and perhaps now, after the much-trumpeted, enigmatical expedition to Lhassa and the unexpected sudden retreat from that city, they will be no better than before.

I was unable to accede to the request of the natives to remain to protect their village, as I intended going farther; and, moreover, the Government of India having become alarmed at my proceeding a second time towards Tibet, behaved with a considerable amount of amusing childishness. Government *chaprassis* were arriving in quick succession with secret orders to prevent natives selling me provisions, to induce my men treacherously to abandon me, steal my weapons and food, and place every possible obstacle in my way.

Some native friends, who, according to custom, had presented me with a ball of *ghur* and two handfuls of rice, were arrested and prosecuted, being brought down to Almora, some 145 miles, for the purpose. Others met with considerable annoyance, accusations of all kinds being showered upon innocent people—even such gross nonsense as accusations of hiding quick-firing guns and pieces of ordnance!

Both the Governor and the Commissioner at Naini-Tal, and the Deputy Commissioner of Almora, seemed quite hysterical over the affair, and some absurd threatening letters were written to me. My mails were invariably tampered with, and all letters opened. Among the most amusing requests may be noted one that I should show a Chinese passport if I wanted to traverse Bhot (British territory), which made it seem as if the cession of that territory to Tibet had really been accomplished—although even then, as I unfortunately experienced before, a Chinese Imperial passport has as much effect upon Tibetan officials as a piece of waste-paper would on the Prime Minister of Great Britain.

I was ordered to divulge my plans, which of course I refused to do, principally because I had no plans to divulge; and, further, was told I must stop and "wait for Government orders." I replied that, being nobody's servant, I would receive no one's orders. I had not asked nor wished nor needed Government assistance, and I would go when and where I liked.

I was very sorry that the Political frontier Agent—a most sensible man—was subjected to much inconvenience and anxiety by constant orders to stop my expedition by any means—a matter in which I also happened to be concerned. He could not, as ordered, starve out my expedition, because I had plenty of food of my own. Silly as the orders given him were, he obediently did his utmost to check my movements, and, moreover, behaved like a gentleman into the bargain.

Some spies whom I found in my camp came in

for some severe punishment, and two Government *chaprassis*, who had one night been despatched to threaten my men and induce them to desert and capture my food and ammunition, received a sound thrashing, were disarmed, and I took them prisoners and brought them along with me to do some mountaineering! At the same time I sent word to those in authority that, when it should suit me, on my return, I would personally hand over the two prisoners.

Further orders arrived that any one selling or giving food or showing friendship to me should be arrested and sent down to Almora for punishment. All this seemed very useless, as I possessed all I needed; but, in order to prevent further persecution to some of my friends, I decided to cross the boundary at once—the Kali River—and enter the Nepal kingdom—a country also closed to foreigners, as everybody knows.

CHAPTER V

In the meantime the Tibetans, who had hastily retreated across the boundary into their country, had given the alarm of the approach of my expedition. A spy I had sent over reported that great commotion reigned at Taklakot. Bridges had been hastily destroyed, stone barriers were put up, while warlike preparations of all kinds were carried on in feverish speed. A bluffing message was sent over by the Tibetans to inform the Political Agent that 5000 men were ready to meet my force and capture me again, when they would cut off my head and throw my body into the river—a threat which was by no means new to me.

This sounded interesting, only the Tibetans forgot that they would have to catch me first! The passes—both the Lippu and the Lumpiya (through the latter of which I had evaded their vigilance on my first journey)—were, they stated, strongly guarded. I well knew the contemptible cowardice of the Tibetans, and I took but little notice of these threats; for this time—unlike my first journey—I had twenty men, all of my own selection, and they were magnificent fellows—faithful and plucky to quite an unusual degree.

In answer to these Tibetan messages to the Government, it is possibly of some interest to notice that the Government of the North-West Provinces in all haste informed the authorities of Taklakot in words to this effect:—

"Mr. Landor is coming to Tibet. Possibly he will enter the country. The Government of India has taken steps to prevent any men accompanying him, also to take away his baggage, provisions, arms, and ammunition. He will enter alone and will be at your mercy. We [the Government] are in no way responsible for his entering Tibet."

This message surprised me even less than the Tibetan effort. Indeed, I well knew that no one more than some officials of the North-West Provinces wished me dead. You see, I had on several occasions shown them up in a very poor light, and now again I was discovering fresh and most unaccountable misdeeds on their part all along the line. Naturally, I quite understood that it was an

RED LAMAS

A. Hy. Savage Landor

uneasy conscience and the fear of being exposed which prompted them to act in such a childish manner in order to prevent my seeing what was going on.

The Political Agent, who was constantly receiving orders which he was powerless to carry out, such as arresting me,—which I defied him to do,—seemed in much distress, and to relieve the strain upon him I decided to cross over into forbidden Nepal territory. The British authorities had taken the precaution to warn the Nepalese also that I might cross over their boundary, that my conduct was not countenanced by the Government, and that soldiers must be sent to stop me and possibly capture me. This led to some incidents which gave us a good deal of unexpected merriment.

A guard of Nepalese soldiers was hurried up, and, unaware that it was there, I crossed over the boundary, with our rifles in their cases for protection against the rain, and not at all prepared for war. Two of my men, who carried a rifle each, were a distance ahead. On nearing a small fort and guard-house they were pounced upon by Nepalese soldiers who were hiding behind some rocks, the rifles were seized, and the Nepalese escaped with them into the fort up higher upon the hill.

My men ran back to me in a great state of excitement to report the occurrence. We hurriedly prepared a plan of attack, and without losing any time climbed up to the fort. Upon the walls some gaily attired figures peeped over, brandishing *kukris* and a few obsolete rifles. I could hear them behind strengthening the hastily barricaded door. An officer peeped over and asked what we wanted.

"I want my rifles back."

"Your rifles are not here. We have already despatched them to Katmandu" (the capital of Nepal).

"Very good. If you do not return my rifles within two minutes we will come and get them ourselves."

"We will fight you."

"All right."

Pounding with big rocks and by the aid of a wooden lever we got the door loosened, and while the garrison's attention was directed to prevent our entering that way, four of my best men and I climbed over the wall on the opposite side of the fort and covered the defenders with our rifles. I demanded that they should lay down their weapons or I would shoot. After some indecision, most of them did. The others, especially one who fired at

TIBETAN MAN SPINNING WOOL

A. H. SAVAGE LANDOR

us, got a severe pounding and were disarmed by my men, who had now all entered the fort.

We ransacked the place, and eventually recovered the captured rifles, after which we bade the Nepalese a respectful salaam and proceeded on our way.

"But," humbly put in the trembling Nepalese, "you cannot travel on Nepal territory. It is forbidden to foreigners, and I have orders to stop you."

"Very well, do it!"

"I cannot," he meekly mumbled, as he rubbed aching bruises he had received in the encounter. "But," he said, "I will follow your movements."

"Oh, you can follow any movements you like, but mind you do not come too near."

"Oh, no, no, *sahib*!" he exclaimed.

The guard, in fact, followed us for some days—and always at a most respectful distance—until we got high up among the snows and glaciers. Then we lost sight of them. Anyhow, I had no further annoyance all through my journey in Nepal, and found the few natives we saw quite attractive, picturesque, and kind.

After leaving the fort we travelled practically south-east over very rough country, my objective being to visit and if possible climb one of the Lumpa peaks which towers in a majestic needle above most other mountains in the neighbourhood. Every now and then, when we got to some higher point of vantage, we got a beautiful view of it. My men—to my astonishment—received my plan with enthusiasm, for they seemed to hold the snows in veneration. Little they then knew how much they would have to suffer upon them,

In that portion of North-West Nepal the population is sparse and somewhat mixed. Perhaps the finest and most interesting types I saw were the cross-breeds of Shokas and Nepalese, which seemed to produce most striking heads. One of the coloured drawings representing a typical Nepalese-Shoka young man, with temples shaved and long wavy hair hanging down his back, is, I think, a good example. These men had very fine traits about them, were most hospitable and civil, manly and serious in manner. They were enterprising traders, carrying on a brisk business mainly in borax, salt, wool, and skins, which they generally bartered with Tibetans in exchange for grain, *ghur*, and other food stuffs.

It is rather interesting to note that whereas similar frontier tribes on neighbouring British soil

A NEPALESE SHOKA

A.H. SAVAGE LANDOR

are imposed upon, taxed and ill-used by Tibetans, no interference at all is experienced by those living under the protection of the King of Nepal. Possibly this is due to the fact that when Nepalese subjects have been ill-used in Tibet an armed expedition has been sent over the frontier by the Nepalese, and reparation demanded and obtained at once.

Nepalese women are not unattractive, having large brown eyes, made additionally languid by blackening the lower lid, long eyelashes and well-cut features, skin of a well-polished, smooth, light-yellowish brown, and most graceful hands and feet. The better class are generally much decorated with heavy silver necklaces, bracelets, and rings, and with huge nose-rings of gold, brass, or silver. They are handsome while young, but they fade away at an early age, and the smooth skin becomes wrinkled and grooved long before they are thirty. They are said to be most affectionate, and of a somewhat jealous temperament, which they couple with extreme conjugal fidelity.

In Western Nepal the hair is worn in many little plaits festooned on both sides of the forehead, and a head-cover, white, yellow, or red, such as is seen in India among Hindoo women, is usually worn.

The women have comparative freedom, and

seldom are they seen completely veiled. *Sati* or *suttee*, the widow's self-sacrifice by throwing herself upon the flames which have cremated her dead husband, is now forbidden by law in Nepal. It is, nevertheless, indulged in to some extent in districts far away from the capital.

Nepal is principally known to English people as the country from which, by a special agreement, we draw recruits for our Gurkha regiments. It should, nevertheless, be borne in mind that not all people living in Nepal are by any means Gurkhas —far from it. We find in Nepal a great variety of types—some pure enough, others distinct mixtures of two or more races.

The Gurkha district proper lies in the northeasterly portion of the Gandak basin, the chief city being Gurkha, some fifty-four or fifty-five miles to the west of the Nepalese capital, Katmandu.

Formerly Nepal's sovereignty extended over Kumaon, which we have already traversed, as far as the Sutlej River. The Nepal kingdom, as it stands now, is an elongated tract of country—mostly mountainous—some 500 miles in length, and less than 150 miles in breadth at its widest points. As everybody knows, it is situated on the southern slopes of the central Himahlyan range, and borders with Tibet on the north, Kumaon (North-West Provinces) to the west, the Kali River, as we know, forming the boundary; the North-West Province and Bengal to the south, and Sikkim to the east.

Nepal is divided into three natural zones by high ranges with peaks rising from 25,000 to 28,000 feet, these ridges shooting off southwards from the main Himahlyan range. The eastern zone is drained by the Kosi River, the central by the Gandak, and the Western by the Gogra. To the above should be added what is called the Terai and the thickly-populated Nepal Valley, which, geographically, must be classed separately. Formerly Nepal was divided into twenty-four principalities in addition to the Gurkha kingdom, but since the invasion by the latter of the entire country they have been divided into five provinces—viz. Gurkha, Malibam, Palpa, Pokra, and Khachi.

In the space at my disposal I cannot enter into the history nor go into a detailed description of the many tribes which inhabit Nepal, but generally speaking, in the aboriginal stock a Mongolian origin is evident, particularly in the population of the central zone, where recent Tibetan influence is marked; but this is not the case with the inhabitants of the lower region, who seem to have descended partly from a mixture of an earlier Tibetan and Aryan source. Perhaps among the most prominent aboriginal tribes we should mention the Magars, Gurungs, Newars, Sunwars, the Khambas or Khambus, and Yakhas (the latter two closely resembling Rais), the Yakthumbas, Murmis, and Lepchas. Then in the forests of Western Nepal we find to this day wild tribes of Chepangs and Kasundas.

In the Terai district live the Tarus, a servile and ill-shaped people of no great strength of character; in the eastern zone we have Limbus, a name which practically includes Kirantis, Ekas, and Rais—a people of apparently Tibetan origin, flat-faced, beardless, and with long unplaited hair, who wear wide trousers and a short jacket instead of the long coat of the Lepchas.

The central zone, from which most of the recruits for the British Gurkha regiments are drawn, is inhabited by a small but strongly built, warlike, and plucky people, the Magars and Gurungs, the Magars being in their turn subdivided into six distinct tribes, of which the Thapa tribe is the most numerous. Both the Magars and the Gurungs—who are somewhat taller and more

A NEPALESE LADY

A.H. SAVAGE LANDOR

stoutly built than the Magars—although of marked Mongolian characteristics, are by religion Brahmins, but have no sort of strong caste prejudices such as one finds, for instance, in India. Gay and simple-minded, with hearts of gold, faithful and obstinate to an extreme degree, independent in themselves yet loyal to their friends or employers, fond of fighting and possessing the courage of lions, these fellows make wonderful soldiers indeed. Perhaps in many ways they are not unlike the Japanese, both in appearance and temperament, except that the physique of the Gurkha is the superior of the two.

In the Valley of Nepal—or Nepal proper—we find mostly Newars and Murmis. The Newars, who claim to be the aborigines of the Nepal Valley, are in many ways not unlike the Bhotias or Shokas, and in many of their customs and in their habitations show a marked similarity to those tribes of Mongolian descent. Their language resembles Tibetan, and their religion is a modified form of inherited Buddhism. The Newars are much given to agricultural pursuits, and they do not display so prominently the fighting qualities of the Magars and Gurungs. On the contrary, they seem to devote all their energy to art and trade, of which they seem to have the entire monopoly in Nepal. The Murmis resemble Bhotias even more closely than the Newars. They are subdivided into two classes — the Barathamang, which is the most numerous, and the Atharajat.

Katmandu, the capital of Nepal and residence of the King and Government, lies in this valley, and is a city of great size and some beauty.

The Terai is inhabited by a poor, sickly-looking race called the Tarus, malarial fever being rampant in their district, while wild beasts abound in the jungle. They seem to be a poverty-stricken lot with a wretched *physique*—although endowed with astounding strength and powers of endurance. They divide their time between fishing, agriculture, and hunting wild animals.

Now comes the western zone, which is entirely inhabited by non-Gurkha tribes, such as the Doti and Jumli (the Doti's country being south of the Jumli's), as well as by wilder tribes, such as the Chepangs and Kusundas, the former being very similar to the Raots or Rajis of Kumaon. Then there are minor Hinduised tribes generically known as Parbatiyas (or hill men).

CHAPTER VI

THE religion, customs, manners, and fashions of dress of the various tribes composing the population of Nepal vary to quite a considerable extent, and I have here not the space to go into them fully. But I will quote a few.

The Brahmins differ little from their co-religionists of India, except that they are not so strict in the observance of prejudices; the form of Buddhism practised closely resembles that of Tibet. Superstitions are rampant, both among Brahmins and Buddhists, and of course even more so among the wilder tribes.

The Gurkhas, on the occasion of the birth of a child, indulge in rejoicings for eleven consecutive days, the father being restricted to the company of his relatives only. On the eleventh day a name is given to the offspring. The child is suckled by the mother for a comparatively short period of time, when a festival and dinner are given, the child being made to swallow a grain of rice from each friend.

Marriages are, as in India, arranged at a very early age, sometimes when children are not more than six or seven years old, the betrothal taking place a year or two before. Widows cannot marry again, but a widower can. Divorces can be obtained in some tribes, by somewhat simple methods, but fidelity is one of the chief virtues of Nepalese women, and it is seldom that separation takes place. Besides, divorces are a very expensive luxury. Moreover, an unfaithful wife may find herself in prison for life, whereas the co-respondent is handed to the mercy of the husband, who is expected to "chop him up" in public with his vicious-looking *kukri*. They say that the offender's life may be spared if he submits to crawl under the husband's leg, raised for the occasion, a most humiliating alternative seldom accepted.

As in India, among Brahmin tribes, a great many misdeeds of vanity or breaches of caste-rules are forgiven on payments in cash to the priests, or the giving of the usual feast and feed.

The custom of shaving the head, moustache,

and eyebrows in sign of mourning at the death of near relations is followed by the Brahmin tribes, and the body of the deceased is buried and not cremated. Several non-Brahmin tribes, however, cremate their dead.

The Gurkhas who are recruited for the British army are nearly all Magars and Gurungs, they being considered the best fighting material. Members of the Khas tribe are enlisted solely for the 9th Gurkha regiment. Recruiting parties are sent out from every regiment which recruits for itself, and these bring down their recruits to the dépôt at Garakpur. Here a primary medical inspection takes place, and clothing is issued to the men before they are despatched to their future corps. They wear a dark green uniform with black or red facings, and are armed with Martini-Henry rifles, a bayonet, and a *kukri*.

The Gurkha Brigade consisted in 1899 of the 1st, 2nd, 3rd, 4th, 5th, 9th, 42nd, 43rd, and 44th Regiments. The first five regiments have two battalions; the 9th, 42nd, 43rd, 44th are single battalions. There are eight British officers to each battalion (*plus* some others attached), a medical officer, and sixteen Gurkha officers.

The men are, as a rule, excellent shots, fond of

sport of all kinds, and passionate fishermen and *shikaris*, knowing instinctively and intimately the habits of most animals. They are hardy, cheery, and willing to obey, but detest "nagging." They are devoted to their officers and proud of their corps; and, taking things all round, possibly they may be put down as the most loyal native troops we have in India. They know no fear. If an orderly were by chance to leave an officer dead or wounded, either in the field or out on a sporting expedition, he would lose his caste, be generally boycotted, and very likely killed by his comrades.

The Gurkhas are inveterate gamblers and fond of all games, showing great quickness in learning British games, at which they become quite proficient—football particularly.

They are superstitious beyond measure, good or evil spirits playing an important part in every day's occurrences. Thus astrologers find plenty of remunerative occupation in predicting events and showing how to propitiate certain demons rather than others.

A curious feature of these fighters is their tender affection for flowers. Indeed, there are many tender strings to the heart of a Gurkha. They are devoted to their families, and most gentle and suave

A NEPALESE WOMAN

A. Hy Savage Landor

in their home manners. They are jealous of their women, whom they do not beat nor usually turn into beasts of burden like the natives of India, and they show great pride in displaying their women-folks loaded with jewellery from head to foot. The women are quite pretty, cheery, and do not exhibit the affected shyness of the women of the Indian plains, for instance.

One of the most notable features about a Gurkha is the marvellous skill with which he handles his heavy-bladed *kukri*. It may be said that from the days of his childhood, since as soon as his little hands become strong enough to lift one, he is never without one; hence, when older, he is very adept in its manifold uses. With one of those knives Gurkhas can cut a buffalo's head off at one stroke; and they can make fairly good shots, at considerable distance, when throwing the *kukri*. They can use it in such delicate work as shaping a toothpick or sharpening a pencil. With it they chop firewood, and use it freely as a cooking utensil.

When going bear-hunting they wind a blanket round the left arm and carry a loaded stick in the right hand, the *kukri* being held between the teeth or thrust in the girdle in front. When the bear gets on his hind-legs to close with them, they hit him on the nose (being the tenderest spot), and, before he has time to recover from the pain and astonishment, they polish him off with their knives.

They delight in the company of tame animals, such as dogs or birds. They are fond of smoking and drinking—and they can stand a lot—a fact which makes them great chums with British white soldiers. They simply adore Tommy Atkins, especially if he be a Highlander or a rifleman, and they delight in his company; but they show the utmost contempt—racial and general—for the natives of India. Their unbounded conceit is easily forgiven and counterbalanced by their extreme truthfulness and honesty, especially when first recruited.

Many Gurkha regiments have for some years taken up the system of training a few picked men of good *physique* and sight, and of unusual agility and sporting instincts, as recognised scouts. They are clad more lightly than ordinary soldiers—generally in "cut short" football knickers. Besides the scouts' duty of discovering the enemy's strength and position, they are also used as sharpshooters, and specially instructed for stalking "snipers" at night. When in India I had the pleasure of

A TYPICAL NATIVE OF N.W. NEPAL

inspecting the scouts commanded by Lieutenant G. Kendall Channer, of the 1st Battalion 3rd Gurkhas, and I was much impressed by them and by the business-like qualities of the officers and men.

CHAPTER VII

At the village of Chongur in Nepal I was able to purchase some extra blankets and shoes for my men, as from this point we should soon come among the snows, where we should remain for some time. Up to an altitude of 11,000 feet we travelled among firs, and on very sharp, slippery slopes without a trail. On a bit of level pasture-land we came across two Jumli *annuals* or shepherds with some sheep. They were curious types, wild and unkempt, with shaggy hair flowing upon their face and shoulders. I do not think that I have ever seen men more *abruti*—to use a French expression which fits them perfectly—than those two. Shivering from cold, ill-clad, living on roots and whatever they could pick up, which was not much, they were indeed the very picture of misery and wretchedness. When they had recovered from their fright at our approach, I gave them some food which would last them some time, and their gratitude knew no bounds.

Farther on we met a Nepalese woman carrying a child slung in a basket upon her back, while the husband walked peacefully behind. When the camera was pointed at the couple they were so disturbed that the woman dropped basket and child and took to her heels down a most precipitous slope, while her better half ran away from us, also full speed, but on a less dangerous route.

Farther on, as we got higher up, we encountered more shepherds, in as pitiable a condition as the first we had seen, having nearly lost their power of speech through leading a lonely life among these mountains. They all suffered from fever and rheumatism; some from goitre through drinking snow water.

The marching was very heavy, especially for my men who carried loads; my pony, of course, had to be abandoned long before this, and I had sent him down to lower elevations in charge of my *sayce*.

We were now nearing the magnificent Api Mountain, and we soon came to the moraine of the glacier. We reached the glacier—which I named the Elfrida Landor Glacier—at sunset, and it was indeed a most beautiful sight with its huge walls of clear ice in irregular terraces, portions only being in broken-up heaps. At the sides, mud of a greyish colour and broken ice bordered the worn, eroded rock down to the level of the valley where the glacier lies.

The glacier lies from N.E.E. to S.W.W., with two high peaks, one to the N.N.W., the other to the S.S.E., the latter being known as the Api Mountain. Two snow-fed streams descend from the glacier, and, joining into a rapid torrent, become a tributary of the Lumpa River. The natives call all these glaciers by the generic term *Sho-gal*, or "snow glacier."

The village of Chongur could be distinguished in the far distance to the N.W. of us, down, down below in the valley of the Kali; and to the N.N.W. we obtained a panoramic view of the Kuti River valley, with the conical Bitroegoar Mountain and a high peak to the N.N.E. Even below 13,000 feet the vegetation had become very sparse, but patches of short grass were found up to 16,000 feet. Above that all was absolutely barren, and generally covered with snow. In the high valley we had followed, whatever trees we found were weather-beaten and half-burnt by the snow and cold winds of the winter months. For long distances we occasionally

ELFRIDA LANDOR GLACIER, NEPAL

walked on thick beds of wild strawberries. These high valleys are considered good pasture-land by the Shokas, who send their sheep for grazing in charge of *annuals*, such as those we had met.

The foot of the glacier where we pitched our tent was at an elevation of 13,900 feet, and the temperature shortly before sunset not higher than 33° Fahrenheit.

Perhaps to those who have never slept on the ice of a glacier it may be interesting to know what it feels like. Barring a certain chilliness which anybody can imagine, a first night on a glacier has many surprises. I say "first night," because we spent a great many, and we got accustomed to the weird noises which kept us awake and in some suspense on the first visit. Indeed, a Himahlyan glacier seems to be the home of noises of all kinds. The wind blowing among the pinnacles and recesses produces weird melodies like solos and immense choruses of human voices; you can hear shrill whistling all round you when sharper blades of ice cut the current of air, and roars like those of wild beasts, only stronger, when the wind penetrates into some deep cavity. No sooner were you closing your eyes again for a much-wanted sleep than thunder, so loud that it made you jump, startled you, but when you peeped out of the tent there were brilliant stars and a limpid sky everywhere above you. Sleepy as you were, you could not resist—at least, I could not, and I am not much of a star-gazer—the temptation to gaze at the stars and planets. In the rarefied and limpid air they showed like huge diamonds, and gave quite enough light to see all round one, even when there was no moon. Indeed, no one who has never been to exceptionally high elevations has an idea of the beauty of stars. They appear several times larger than they do when seen from London or Paris, for instance, and the magnificence of their ever-changing colours is indescribable.

Well, there was poetry enough in that, but you were soon awakened from your contemplation by some unexpected explosion which made you think the whole landscape before you must have been blown up. But no, there were no visible signs of commotion around. It was merely a new crevasse, some hundreds of feet deep, splitting, for some reason, climatic or other, in the ice. Constant rumblings you heard, near and distant; and you only had to close your eyes and you could imagine yourself in a forest with the wind rustling among the trees, or the pleasant sound of a waterfall close by, or an æolian harp being played by a divine hand.

Echoes, of course, there are by the dozen on mountains, and each sound is repeated over and over again till it fades away. An occasional boulder gets loose from the rotted rock up on the mountain side, and is precipitated with bounding leaps on to the ice of the glacier; a huge one weighing some tons came down that night and missed our tent by not very many yards. My men said the spirits of the mountains were doing all this for our special benefit, to see whether we were brave or not! The big boulder they had flung at and purposely missed us to show us their powers, but not to hurt us. This was a good sign. "The gods are with us," they stated; but internally I heartily prayed that we might have no more "good signs" of that nature.

While I was trying to make some hot chocolate with a small spirit-stove, my men were busy packing up, they bearing the discomfort with some considerable pluck. We had not been able to make a fire, and we had not the prospect of seeing many for some weeks to come. I always found chocolate the most useful and sustaining food for mountaineering purposes, and I carried any number of tablets in my pockets. On the march I constantly ate it; food, I found, keeping one's strength up and being more easily digested under those circumstances, if spread in small quantities over the entire day, than if eaten in large quantities twice or three times a day at given hours. I had my chocolate specially prepared with a percentage of meat and fat, which gave it additional nourishment. For days and days at a time I lived on chocolate only, it being impossible to cook food, and deeming it rather dangerous to eat tinned meats cold.

I was able to overcome the caste scruples of my men, and they, too, partook freely of my chocolate, although I never let them know that it contained beef. Had they known this, most of them would have lost their caste. They ate it because they believed it entirely prepared by machinery and not touched by unclean hands!

I was sorry when we struck camp and left behind the beautiful glacier and Api Mt., 19,919 feet. We soon rose over a pass (13,050 feet) where we obtained a view of a second glacier, almost as fine as the first, in precipitous terraces, and with a gigantic terminal moraine, covered in great part by *débris* and rotten rock, fallen from

FUNNELS IN THE MORAINE ICE

the mountain at the side. This I called the Armida Glacier. It spread in a direction from N.E. to S.W. To the west of the glacier on the mountain side there was hardly any snow up to 16,000 feet, but to the east, as one looked towards it, there were huge masses.

The entire valley of the Lumpa river along which we were travelling made part of a gigantic glacier, with side glaciers such as those we have seen. In the lower portion of the valley the ice was covered with *débris.*

At the foot of the Armida Glacier were some immense parallel crevasses in the ice. The upper portion of these was a mixture of dark grey mud and rock embedded in the ice, showing vertical streaks and corrugations. Then there were some curious pits in the moraine, such as the one shown in the illustration, funnel-shaped and of great depth, some 60 feet deep and more, and about 100 feet in diameter. These funnels, cone-shaped, had a great fascination—quite an irresistible attraction—when one looked into them. The ice, of a beautiful light green colour, was corrugated into grooves converging towards the centre at the bottom, where a deep hole was generally to be found. The ridges of the myriads of grooves reflected in a line of silver the rays of the sun, and these many dazzling luminous streaks all converging towards one point had quite an hypnotic effect on some of my more highly strung men. One man became quite giddy in looking down, and very nearly went over, and several other men experienced a strong desire to precipitate themselves into these pits.

I puzzled my head a great deal to find out exactly how these funnels were produced, and the only plausible explanation seemed that some boulder fallen from the mountain side had, owing to its sun-absorbed high temperature, gradually bored a hole into the ice. The walls of the cylindrical hole, becoming in their turn exposed to the strong sunlight, went through a process of melting, the heat affecting the upper portion to a much greater extent than farther down, where the strength of the sun's rays would be mitigated by the influence on the temperature of the air by the surrounding ice. Thus the quicker melting of the upper portion compared with the lower would at once have a tendency to produce the conical shape of the funnels.

Then, of course, the grooves in the ice are produced by the water of the melting surface ice

THE ARMIDA LANDOR GLACIER,
NEPAL

flowing down. In fact, in the daytime, the lower centre hole, which had vertical walls, was almost invariably filled with water.

Perhaps, to avoid the absurd criticisms of fault-discovering critics (which criticisms arise merely from their own appalling and fantastic ignorance), it may be as well to remind the reader that the sun's rays, even at very great elevations and among quantities of snow and ice, can be very powerful—85°, 90°, and even more. This particularly if the region in which one is travelling is, as was that where we were, in a latitude north of 30° 4′ 0″ only from the Equator. Naturally, the drop in the temperature when the sun disappears is enormous, from 60° to 100° being nothing very exceptional. This also applies in a lesser degree between the sun and shade in the daytime. When marching, for instance, due north or south in those regions, it is not unusual to have one's anatomy roasting on the side where it is struck by the sun, and to be half-frozen on the other side.

We continued our journey upon the moraine of the main glacier, avoiding as much as we could the dangerous cracks and treacherous holes. Half-way up the main glacier we were at an altitude of 18,600 feet. On descending some 400 feet we came to a plain wherein grew rhubarb and some turnips, the former wild, the latter planted by Nepalese shepherds. There were, in fact, three tiny shelters of stones and mud where the poor wretches had lived. We were much rejoiced at finding some shrubs we could use as fuel. The glacier we were leaving behind was separated from this valley by a high dune of mud and *débris.*

After crossing a stream we came to a third, the Martia Glacier, some 15,500 feet above sea-level. This glacier was not quite so impressive as the other two, but it was, nevertheless, a most beautiful basin filled with masses of clear ice in irregular terraces. A great moraine extended here across the valley from the glacier, forming a ridge which we had to climb in order to proceed on our journey. There seemed to be traces of iron in the *débris* of the moraine as well as in the rocks of the mountains around, and upon the gigantic boulders which had been shot down upon the ice.

On the opposite side of the Lumpa stream to the one on which we stood, just before reaching the third glacier, were high vertical rocks of brilliant colouring. To the south-east of the glacier at the foot was the usual dune, and we again found a great many gigantic pits, all with water at the bottom.

We came to a very dangerous crevasse which we could not cross, and we had to make a considerable detour. The edge on which we had got seemed on the point of giving way, and might have collapsed at any moment. Where the surface ice was covered by *débris* it showed graceful undulations and well-rounded mounds, but occasionally there were higher hillocks of conical shape and quite pointed.

Still travelling upon the moraine of the Lumpa Glacier we arrived at last at the spot where the Lumpa river has its birth, dripping gently from the glacier. Here, too, the ice with the overlying *débris* showed in its general lines the peculiar sweeping curves noticeable in all these glaciers, the section to the east being, in this particular glacier, an exception to the rule, and exhibiting a disorderly mass of *débris* and huge blocks of ice.

We had reached a point where a bifurcation occurred, one arm of the glacier extending to 160° bearings magnetic (S.S.E.), the other and principal one to 120° bearings magnetic, towards the Lumpa Mountain.

We selected this spot to make our camp, and a very cold camp it was, too. We pitched our tent alongside a big rock, and with fuel we had brought up, tried, after sundown, to make a fire inside the tent in order to keep ourselves warm. But we were nearly suffocated by the smoke. During the night, while my men were asleep—and the fire gone out—I changed the plates in three magazine cameras, forty-eight plates altogether; a job which with semi-frozen and trembling fingers, and careful packing of negatives already exposed, took me the best part of two hours. Indeed, one of the great tortures of exploration in cold climates, is the immense care with which one must nurse one's surveying and other instruments under most adverse circumstances, and the inexpressible trouble which photography, if done seriously, involves. For similar kind of work I always found plates infinitely more reliable than films; but, of course, with them the use of a red lantern becomes imperative, and often leads to the use of a good deal of bad language. If you adopt an oil-lantern the oil gets frozen into a solid mass, and it is somewhat troublesome to keep the lantern burning, whereas candles have other disadvantages. As for feeling the film side with your fingers, and changing plates in the dark, it is, of course, out of the question when your hands are too cold.

Maybe another hint when mountaineering at

AUTHOR'S CAMP, NEPAL

great altitudes will be useful to you. Never use a waterproof sleeping-bag, such as those you see advertised and recommended, as the very thing you want on a mountain. If you do, and the night is a cold one, you will find yourself and your blankets soaked in condensed moisture from the heat of your body coming in contact with the cold waterproof sheet, through which it is unable to escape. Of course it is wise to use a waterproof sheet to lie on under one's blankets.

On that particular night, feeling extra cold and not thinking of consequences, I wrapped myself up, over my blankets, in a waterproof. The results were disastrous. Everything got drenched, and, when I got up, blankets and clothes became solid sheets of ice!

CHAPTER VIII

HAVING seen that all my instruments were in good condition, I selected about a dozen of my strongest men to accompany me on my ascent on one of the Lumpa peaks. It had been sleeting and snowing during the night, and when I roused my men shortly before five in the morning there was a thick mist which seemed to penetrate to the very marrow of one's bones. With chattering teeth and a chilly nose, we got all things ready, and brewed a parting cup of hot tea, after which we set out on our errand, the other men remaining to take care of the camp.

Every now and then the wind cleared the mist, and we could see a bright, clear sky above us which gave us hope that we might have a fine day. I am not a believer in early rising; as a rule eight or nine o'clock is my favourite hour for starting on a march, when the sun is already high above the horizon. You then start off in comfort, instead of waking with an angry feeling that you are being done out of some hours' sleep. On this occasion, however, we had such a long distance to cover, and in all probability troublesome and dangerous marching before us, that I wished to have as many hours of daylight before me as possible.

No sooner had we started, following the main glacier in a direction of 120°, than a thick fog set in which made progress somewhat troublesome. It seemed to get thicker and thicker as we were rising higher upon the glacier. We had to find our way among numerous pits and crevasses. We kept as close together as was practicable, but we were not roped together. It has ever been my rule when mountaineering that every man must look after himself. I take all sensible precautions to avoid all accidents, and collective accidents in particular. If there has to be a mishap, which is not likely, and some unfortunate man slips into a crevasse, do not let him by any means drag down the whole party, as is frequently the case when roped together. Besides, the rope in itself is a great hindrance to one's progress, and on very rough marching exhausts much of the traveller's strength, being either too tight or too slack, and always getting in the way when it should not.

We tramped along as best we could over a great many transverse waves of ice, covered here and there with *débris*—most fatiguing work. In the first portion of the main glacier, on which we were, and which lay from W. to E., the transverse waves followed a parallel direction of N.W. to S.E. until we reached an altitude of 15,000 feet with a temperature of 42° ; but in the upper part of the glacier, which lay from N.W. to S.E., these parallel waves lay in a direction of from S.W. to N.E. In the higher portion of the glacier, 15,400 feet above sea-level, we came to a regular maze of huge pits in close succession, and we were glad when the sun shone brightly on us and little by little dispelled the fog, so that we could see what we might expect ahead of us.

On our left we had precipitous mountains of grey rock ; on our right somewhat gentler slopes, mostly covered with snow. We at last reached the crescent-shaped Lumpa basin, walled all round with two higher peaks joined by a semicircular high barrier of snow-clad rock.

We were particularly fortunate as we approached. The mist lifted like the curtain of a theatre and

ONE OF THE LUMPA PEAKS AND PART OF THE CHARLES LANDOR GLACIER

This picture shows how feathery clouds form on mountain slopes at elevations above 23,000 feet, and disposes of certain scientific theories that no clouds can exist at such great altitudes.

A. H. SAVAGE LANDOR

unexpectedly disclosed a magnificent view before us, brilliantly illuminated by the light of the sun. I was lucky enough to obtain several excellent photographs and sketches, one giving a panoramic view of the scene being reproduced in this book.

I possess some negatives taken on that occasion that are of particular interest, as showing the idiocy of certain people who maintain that clouds do not form above an altitude of 20,000 feet. The very fact that you find snow up to the summits at Nanda Devi (25,660 feet), and Mt. Everest (29,000 feet), might, I think, be sufficient proof to the contrary to any one except possibly a Royal geographer; but in my negatives the clouds themselves show as they were forming on the summit of one of the Lumpa peaks, which has an elevation of 23,490 feet.

A few negatives of lesser importance were injured owing to a most uncommon occurrence. In my magazine camera the plate-holders were of metal, and slid one on the top of the other when being changed for exposure. Owing to the dryness of the atmospherc the friction of metal on metal produced an electric spark inside the camera, which marked some of the plates across like a streak of lightning, and somewhat fogged them.

Of course, I only discovered this on developing them.

My object in making the ascent of this high peak was not so much for the sake of getting there as for the purpose of making some observations on the effects of great altitudes upon human beings, a subject in which I was then rather interested. We continued climbing upon the glacier until we came to a big stretch broken into huge and tortuous crevasses of immense depth. When you stooped over the edge and looked down, the ice-walls on either side showed most beautiful tints, from intense blue at the bottom fading in most delicious tones to pale green and to the pure white of the surface snow. These crevasses were very wide in some places, but here and there they were close together, and we could easily jump across.

We then left the glacier, and proceeded climbing along the mountain side to our right, upon extensive snow-fields. The first portion of the ascent was in no way difficult, and we proceeded quickly enough considering the great elevation. But on reaching 20,000 feet some of my men were taken with mountain sickness, and they had great difficulty in keeping up with us. They bled considerably from the nose, and were eventually seized

DEEP CREVASSES IN THE GLACIER ICE

with such violent pains that we had to leave them behind—to be picked up on our return. Out of twelve men only four were still in good condition, and having seen to the comfort of the sick men we left them, wrapped up in their blankets, in a sheltered hollow upon the mountain side.

We next came to a patch of very troublesome loose *débris*, so steep that even snow would not stop on it, and we sweated and sweated for some time trying to get on. Every time you took a step you started a mass of *débris*, sliding with a great roar down the mountain side, and you went sliding back yourself almost to where you had moved from.

When we managed to get higher we were among bigger rocks, also quite loose, and it seemed as if the sound of one's voice was sufficient to start dozens of them on a bounding race for lower elevations. We were resting for a while when a lot of these stones came rolling and bounding towards us with great force, and on the loose stuff upon which we stood it was impossible to get out of the way quickly. One big rock particularly came bounding down in such an erratic fashion that we saw its approach with some concern. One of my men, in whose direction it seemed bound, shouted for help and tried to get aside, but he was hit with great vehemence in his legs and sent flying some feet into the air. He was much shaken and bruised, but after some rubbing and thumping he was able to continue.

When we were about to leave the *débris* we witnessed a most attractive sight—a sight which, nevertheless, caused me considerable anxiety for some minutes. It was the birth of an avalanche. Some snow having got loose higher up upon the mountain, it began rolling down in little balls, thousands of them, which got bigger and bigger as you were looking at them, owing to the snow they collected on their precipitate career. The avalanche passed in a furrow only a few yards from us, affording a magnificent view; but this furrow, unhappily, led to the very spot where I had left my sick men, down, down below, and we could see them, as big as ants, lying wrapped in their red blankets on the white snow, unconscious of the approaching danger. The myriad of snowballs, which were no bigger than ping-pong balls when they started, were as big as decent-sized buildings when they had gone some hundreds of yards, and when two of them clashed in their descent it seemed like an explosion of a mine, the scattered

ROCKS OF ALL SIZES ROLLED WITH
GREAT FORCÉ DOWN THE
MOUNTAIN SIDE

snow in powdered form being thrown up to a great height and looking not unlike smoke. The hollow, whirling sound as the avalanche whizzed past was quite impressive, and I must confess that I was never so relieved as when I saw it just miss my invalided men down below, and end its run with a great clash upon the glacier at the bottom. It seemed like heavy thunder when it struck, which was echoed for some minutes in the mountains all round and down the passage through which we had approached the glacier.

When we reached the crest of the range we came to a difficult passage where the rock, just like the blade of a knife, was so sharp and its sides so steep that even the snow would not remain on it. We had to get across somehow, and the only way to do it was to balance oneself on the top of it—less than a foot wide—or, if one's head was not steady enough, proceed astride of it. It was only a few feet long, but the drop, had one fallen, was several thousand feet on either side. Apart from the fact that it was so high, there was no real difficulty in getting across, and, panting and blowing, stopping every few feet for breath, we proceeded higher and higher.

My men were suffering considerably, their hearts

beating in a most irregular fashion with occasional violent throbs, which caused me much anxiety. These throbs, when they occurred, caused such sudden exhaustion that the men fell down half-fainting, and it took some minutes to revive them and bring them further. They were, however, most plucky, and struggled like men, uncomplainingly. They never once asked to give in and go back.

From an altitude of about 22,000 feet their sufferings took a somewhat acute form, nausea and profuse bleeding from the nose causing them much inconvenience. They complained of intense pains and abnormal pressure in the centre of the chest as well as along the fissures in the skull, particularly where the skull is thinner on the top at the point of junction, and at the temples; also of a severe pressure low in the back of the skull. They were much worried over the maddening buzzing caused by the rarefied air, which they heard and could not explain. They attributed it to something having got inside their ears. Their hearing was temporarily affected when we got higher still, and they experienced difficulty in hearing me speak at all.

When we had got to 23,000 feet, my nose, too,

THE BIRTH OF AN AVALANCHE

bled like a fountain, and I could not stop the flow, but, contrary to my expectation, it seemed to cause me relief rather than discomfort. I could breathe more freely, and my heart did not beat in such a reckless manner as before. It caused me a slight pain and pressure on the top of the skull, but nowhere else.

Of course the exhaustion was indescribable. It was all one could do to go four or five yards at a time, although the ascent after a certain point was in no way difficult, because on looking at the mountain I had instinctively chosen the easiest way to go up. One panted so convulsively and the heart beat so hard and quick that it rather made one reflect.

Possibly the most trying consequence of travelling so high up was the weight which one's limbs seemed to assume. One hardly had the strength to lift them up. The effort of moving one's legs in succession three or four times exhausted one temporarily as much as if one had walked thirty miles under ordinary circumstances.

Well, on we struggled, with an occasional grin at our plight. The last few hundred feet of our ascent were indeed hard work.

One of my men, the strongest-looking lad in my

party, who had been panting most terribly and gasping for breath, unluckily burst a blood-vessel when we were within a few feet of the top. He was in intense pain. We screened him in a sheltered nook. He suffered very much, poor fellow, and although on our return we brought him down again, he eventually died.

At last we reached the summit—23,490 feet (measured by me with the hypsometrical apparatus with three different boiling-point thermometers checked at the Kew Observatory before my departure and after my return. Two excellent aneroids which I also carried gave a similar figure within a few feet).

The day was a beautifully clear one up there, but down below there was much mist and many clouds, which took away a good deal from the beauty of the panorama. There were, however, a great many high snowy peaks towering above the mist like majestic white islands rising out of the sea of clouds. The view was soon almost entirely obscured by clouds, and with the exception of Api Mt., to the N.N.W., another peak, 20,280 feet, in Nepal, peeping through to the N.E. of us, one of the Lumpa group and other mountains close by, we could see very little.

A PERILOUS CROSSING

The peak on which we were was in a steep gradient on the side on which we had climbed, but was most precipitous on the other side. In fact, it was almost vertical right down to the glacier at its foot, some 6500 feet below. It looked as if one half of the mountain had at some remote period collapsed, leaving the sharp-edged peak standing. There was not as much snow on the top as lower down, as the wind blows a good deal of the surface snow away, some melts with the heat of the sun, and the slope of the mountain, even on the side we had climbed, being somewhat steep, whenever sufficient snow had accumulated on the top its weight caused it to slide down in avalanches. Even the day I went up we counted some five or six avalanches in various parts of the mountain, but none came quite so near as the first I described.

The rock was exposed in one or two places, and was so rotted that with our fingers we could remove large slabs. When we had taken a good rest, which restored us wonderfully—as soon as you sat down and did nothing you felt well and relatively happy, except the lungs, which seemed not to work quite so regularly—we took advantage of the rock at hand to construct a cairn on the summit. After having inscribed the names of my men and my own on a stone and on a piece of paper, we placed them in a receptacle on the south side of the cairn and built them up all round and above, so that they might be preserved as long as possible.

I then proceeded to take all the necessary observations — not, however, before having devoured two whole pounds of chocolate, which I ate with some snow to allay my thirst as well as my appetite.

I had been consuming on that ascent a great many lozenges of highly concentrated meat,—each one was supposed to be as good as a meal,—and I ate at least fifty in the space of eight hours and a half. I suppose they were sustaining, but you had to eat lots of them for one lozenge to sustain the previous one, or they left an awful feeling of emptiness in one's inside. An empty inside, I firmly believe, is a mistake for reaching high elevations, or at any other time, so I had started with my pockets full of chocolate, and what the lozenges could not do the huge chunks of chocolate I chewed all the way up the mountain certainly accomplished.

I think it was partly due to the constant

nourishment I took all the way up that I was able to break the world's record in mountaineering, going several hundred feet higher than other mountaineers, with comparative ease. Had the peak which we climbed been higher, I could have gone even higher and reached a considerably greater elevation. But perhaps Nature gave me quite an abnormal constitution for work of that kind, as people who know me can testify.

It is interesting to note that the strongest and most athletic-looking man in my party on that particular expedition was the only one who broke down badly and died; and the weakest, smallest-framed—almost girlish in appearance, he looked so delicate—was the only one out of all the followers I had employed who throughout stood the hardships and sufferings without a flinch, showed the greatest endurance, and eventually returned home in excellent condition.

Perhaps I should also mention that neither myself nor any of the men who came up with me wore hobnailed boots in making the ascent, I wearing some comparatively light boots of medium weight such as I would wear in London on a wet day. In the way of clothing, too, I made no difference between going up on a world's record-breaking expedition and taking a stroll down Piccadilly. I mean that I wore my Piccadilly clothes up there—clothes of the thinnest tropical material, no underclothing to speak of, a straw hat, and a small bamboo stick in my hand.

It has always been my practice to simplify everything. One cannot get away from the fact that the simpler you are in everything you do the better, and with mountaineering particularly, the less you carry, the less muffled up you are, the freer in your movements, the more you will accomplish. That is to say, if your constitution is so made that you can stand it.

I cannot get away from the fact that one can do no better than wear such comfortable clothes as one is generally in the habit of wearing, and I could never understand the object of parading in clumsy tweeds strapped all over, when you need your movements as little impeded as possible.

I will refer you to one of the coloured plates, copied from a photograph taken at an altitude of some 20,000 feet on Lumpa by one of my men before we left them on the mountain side. The picture shows the author and the four men who accompanied him to the summit of the mountain.

A. HENRY SAVAGE LANDOR AND THE FOUR MEN WHO ACCOMPANIED HIM ON HIS ASCENT TO 23,490 FEET ABOVE SEA-LEVEL.

This picture is from a photograph taken at an altitude of some 20,000 feet.

A Hy Savage Landor

CHAPTER IX

WE must go back a while in the narrative. On having reached the summit and delivered themselves of the instruments, cameras, etc., which they carried, the men immediately threw themselves down and fell fast asleep, breathing heavily and quite exhausted. I let them rest awhile before taking observations upon them. When I woke them up one by one they did not respond very quickly,—as they usually did,—but seemed to remain for some minutes semi-unconscious, as if they had been under the influence of a narcotic. This was undoubtedly caused by the rarefied air.

On the ascent above 20,000 feet I had noticed how profuse the salivation had been with my men; the saliva glands being most active when the men underwent exertion, but not so much now that they were stationary. Curiously enough, one of the four men who suffered least during the ascent and when up there on the summit was a fellow—a Rajiput by caste—who had never been on a snow mountain in his life. His determined enthusiasm, I think, and strong will helped him to no mean extent.

I am unable to give the men's names here, lest I should expose them to further persecution from the Government of India, but we will call them A, B, C, D.

A, 45 years of age, after a good rest, had a fairly regular heart-beat, but very fast. He felt quite ill, and complained of a severe pressure at the temples and the top of the head. Every two minutes or so his lungs and heart showed some convulsive movements; also abnormal movements were noticeable in the centre of the chest. His pulse registered 105 beats a minute, and was extremely faint, while his temperature was 102°. This was the man who broke a blood-vessel.

B, a Shoka, 50 years old, and who had constantly lived at great elevations, had a stronger pulse, 80 pulsations per minute, with a temperature of 100°·2. His forehead was burning, and he had a strong buzzing in his ears. Pain and convulsive movements in the lungs, and also in the centre of chest, every few breaths.

C, a powerfully-built Shoka, felt abnormal weak-

THE HIGHEST MOUNTAIN ALTITUDE
EVER REACHED BY A HUMAN BEING

(23,490 feet above sea-level). A. Henry Savage Landor and four natives.

A. Henry Savage Landor

ness, although his pulse was only 78, quite regular, but so faint that one could hardly feel it. The heart, too, beat quite feebly but regularly enough, when not exerting himself. He had bled considerably on the ascent. His temperature was 98°. His ears were buzzing, and he suffered from tormenting pressure in the temples, top and back of skull.

D, the Rajiput, astonished me very much. He only had 76 pulsations, very steady and strong, although he had bled profusely; his heart beat violently and throbbed alarmingly every few moments. His respiration was regular, but slightly quicker than normal. He complained of great heat in the head. His forehead was burning; his temples, he said, seemed as if they were being crushed in a claw of iron, and as if his skull would split. He suffered from great pressure in the tenderest spot on the top of his skull and also behind the head. His temperature was 100°·2.

All complained of great heaviness in the legs and arms, of dryness of the skin, particularly at the forehead and lips, and unquenchable thirst. The pupils of the eyes were in all cases abnormally contracted, although the light was not strong at the time of examination.

I was impressed by the distinctness with which sounds travelled; voices sounding extraordinarily clear, quite crystalline, and if loud and near producing quite a sharp and uncomfortable impression upon the tympanum of one's ears, notwithstanding that the rarefied air caused the sensation of having my ears stopped with cotton-wool.

After half-an-hour's rest the observations upon myself were as follows:—120 pulsations per minute, and heart beating at a similar rate, rather stronger than usual, but quite regular. Temperature under tongue 99°·3. The forehead, unlike my men's, quite cool but feeling very dry, and there remained a slight pressure along the fissures at the side of the skull. Both with me and with all my men the temperature of the body around the heart was greatly increased, and we all suffered from an insatiable thirst. We constantly filled our mouths with snow and melted it in order to appease the uncomfortable feeling, but in a moment the palate and throat felt quite dry, although, as I have stated, salivation was profuse, especially while eating or taking exertion.

While my men were busy constructing the cairn I did a very foolish thing. From our pinnacle down to the glacier below in a vertical line was a drop of some 6500 feet, and for some reason or other I took it into my head to go and sit on the edge and dangle my legs over the precipice. You see, one does not always have an opportunity of having so much room to dangle one's legs and feet in! In order to avoid accidents I knocked off some of the surface snow and then, helped by one of my men—who entered fully into the humour of the situation—I sat myself down.

I was gaily kicking my feet about, when my man shouted that the ice and rock were giving way from under me. Before I had time to get up from my unpleasant position the fellow had pluck and sense enough to try and reach over, seizing me firmly by the wrist, and as the rock and ice and snow went from under, not only were my legs dangling over the precipice, but my whole body was suspended in mid-air.

It seems that in his efforts to save me I might have dragged the man down as well, had it not been for the presence of mind of a third fellow who interrupted the construction of our cairn and seized my saviour by the legs. After some dangling about—which seemed to last a very long time—they eventually pulled me up.

Now, had those men been English or Scotch or Irish or French, this incident might have supplied them with some excitement and a topic of conversation for some time. But no; the man B, who had caught me in the first instance, felt with his foot a spot where the snow seemed firm enough, and he placidly remarked: "Sit down here, Sahib, this will not give way," and he sat himself down as if nothing had happened, while the man C resumed the construction of the cairn without any comment.

My heart thumped a good deal from the sudden jerk—not to speak of the prospect of the unexpected flight—but on feeling myself all over and finding that I had not lost anything from my pockets, nor my straw hat, I soon felt quite happy again. A glance at the two sketches illustrating this incident will, I think, give a clearer idea of the situation than the description.

We remained about an hour on our lofty pinnacle, the temperature in the sun being 70°, and then we made our way down. Holding one another by the hand we slid down the steep incline at a precipitous pace. The distance which had taken us hours of toiling and panting in our ascent, only took us a very short time in

WITHIN AN ACE OF BEING
PRECIPITATED SOME 6500 FEET ON TO
THE GLACIER BELOW

the descent. A thick mist was coming on and my men were most anxious to get down quick.

We were sliding down at a terrific rate, using our feet as brakes to control the velocity when it got too dangerous. We eventually found ourselves again on the loose *débris* and here, too, we went down several yards at each step, carrying down with us a mass of loose stones—a regular land-slide—which rolled right down to the bottom with tremendous *fracas.*

As we got lower, we all felt notable relief in breathing, and we halted for a few minutes to pick up the men we had left below. They had obtained a good rest, and were feeling better.

We gave a parting look to the magnificent glacier—which I named the Charles Landor, after my father—and its stupendous irregular terraces of clear ice rising vertically over 1000 feet in height. The terraces were undulating on their summit, and showed a tendency to precipitate towards the southern side.

On our return we followed a simpler plan. The tail of the glacier showed three high ridges of ice, covered farther down with *débris*, these ridges—two lateral and a central one—running practically parallel to each other and being formed by the forcing up of the ice at the sides and in the centre. Also, the snow precipitated from the sides of the mountains would tend to increase their height—while the heat of the mountain rock would cause the snow in its immediate neighbourhood to melt, and thus leave a channel clear between the mountain itself and the dunes thus formed. As there was some snow on the summit of these dunes one got a fair grip with one's feet; and walking upon their summit involved no great difficulty, except that when one had balanced oneself upon them for long distances one occasionally felt a little giddy. This was, nevertheless, a great improvement upon walking down below among the crevasses, holes, and pools, as we had done in the morning, and saved us no end of time and exertion. True enough, if we had slipped we might have shot down with some force into a crevasse with little hope of coming out alive, but we must not slip, that was all. As each of us had to look after himself, we were mighty careful where and how we put our feet.

The central ridge here, as in most other glaciers, was usually higher and sharper-edged than the lateral ones, and had also a more

THE LUMPA BASIN AND CHARLES LANDOR GLACIER

uneven summit, rather like the conventional wave pattern, inverted arcs of a circle coming in contact and forming pointed summits. We travelled on the ridge to our left on leaving the glacier.

At six o'clock in the evening we again reached camp—oh, how glad we were!—having been on the go steadily for thirteen hours, during which time we had covered sixteen miles. This was not at all bad, at such elevations and on such difficult ground. Of course, most of that distance was between the camp and the glacier at the foot of the Lumpa basin; the actual distance from the glacier to the summit, although occupying the greater portion of the time, being comparatively small.

There were great rejoicings in camp that night, and they took the form of an elaborate—but only half-cooked—meal, our fuel giving out in the middle of the cooking. You see, at high elevations water takes such a long time to boil; in fact, it boils without being hot. At that particular camp it boiled at 187°·3—and cooking took an interminable time. With a display before me—and it did not remain a display very long—of tepid Bovril soup, sardines, army ration stew (semi-stewed), corned beef, tinned plum pudding (Lord! it felt heavy even up there!), and a warmish mug of chocolate—I felt as happy again —in fact, happier than a king!

A BALANCING FEAT

CHAPTER X

WE made a very early start again the following morning, as I had the intention of crossing the range to the north of us and exploring some of the virgin glaciers of the Tinker region and in Tibet. The mountains were, however, so precipitous that we had some difficulty in finding a spot where we could climb up and take our loads as well.

We again proceeded upward towards the Charles Landor Glacier, but kept on the dune to the left (going up) instead of on the one we had taken coming down the previous night. Again we passed along huge cracks in the ice, and here and there more holes in the ice—relieving somewhat the monotony of the grey *débris* that covered that tail portion of the glacier. Again we got another distant glimpse of the majestic glacier itself towering in front of us with its gigantic ice-terraces. Perhaps the reason that these terraces droop towards the southern side may be attributed to the heat of the sun shining upon the ice of that side for more hours than on the north side, as the high wall enclosing the basin on the east side casts a shadow upon the glacier until the sun is well up in the sky.

Somehow or other the dune we were on was not as regular as the one of the previous night, and the *débris* which covered it was very loose and slippery. It often crumbled under us, so that we thought we had better march in the deep channel between the mountain side and the dune. Here, too, we had to feel our way with great caution, as the ground was treacherous, with cracks in the ice bridged over with snow and *débris*. This seemed a great day for landslides. At every moment we heard crashing noises of masses of *débris* being precipitated upon the glacier, and some of them were quite near enough for us to see.

The range to the north of us seemed so uninterrupted and so steep everywhere, with a base of rotten *débris*, and high vertical rocks at the summit, that we were quite puzzled to find a spot where we could cross it. I had noticed a

MORAINE OF GLACIER AND MOUNTAINS
SHOWING HOW CLOUDS FORM
ON THE SNOW-LINE

likely—but difficult—place the day before, and it was, indeed, the only accessible way up. We there left the glacier and began a stiff climb on the loose *débris*, my men experiencing much difficulty in conveying their loads up. Every few hundred feet they had to lie down for some minutes to rest. Although the fatigue was really for them overpowering, they took matters in the right spirit, and instead of grumbling they laughed heartily at the difficulty of breathing, and the thumping and throbbing of the heart. We eventually got away from the lower *débris* and proceeded among large slabs of rock, most slippery and troublesome, and as sharp as knives, our feet getting constantly jammed between them. At last we came before a wall of rock, at such a steep angle that it looked almost perpendicular, with cracks and fissures in it, and on this we had to climb, clinging with all our might with fingers and toes. This part of the ascent was quite dangerous, for, had we slipped, it meant certain death. The rock was so cold that one's fingers got semi-frozen; and we felt much relieved when every now and then we found a hollow or crack, or projection, allowing sufficient room to sit down and rest, our legs swinging over the abyss down below. The bringing up the loads gave us no end of trouble, and it was a pleasure to see how thoughtful and helpful my men were to one another.

We eventually got to a spot where we could go neither up nor down, as some of the rock gave way; and it was with some trepidation that we watched one of my Shokas make steps in the rotten rock while clinging with one hand and his toes apparently to nothing. This took a long time, and this difficulty being overcome and a way made, we climbed and climbed on all fours until we reached the pass.

We heartily named it there and then the "Savage Pass." We took a long rest on the summit, and erected two large cairns with our names in them. We obtained a most stupendous view of the glacier we had left behind uncoiling itself several hundred feet below us. It looked very nasty, with its huge cracks and crevasses, and the three dunes all along it, like huge serpents uncoiling themselves. We had hardly time to admire the scenery before we were enveloped in thick mist, to the north of us particularly, the entire landscape being hidden from us. A few moments later it began to snow. Water boiled as low as 182°, while the temperature of the air was 51°, the altitude in feet being 17,331.

Whether because of the reaction after the hard work of getting up there, or because of the sudden cold and depression in the atmosphere, due to the coming storm, a number of my men were taken violently ill with mountain sickness. They wrapped themselves in their blankets, and said they were dying and could not move. After a good deal of persuasion, and some shaking—which is always a good remedy for most complaints—we made a start.

On the other side of the range we were confronted with very much the same sort of ground as what we had found coming up. First now came a wall-like rock precipice to descend—much more difficult always than to ascend; and then the snow falling fast prevented our seeing many feet ahead of us, besides making our hands, ears, and nose unpleasantly cold. We clung to those rocks and went carefully down, the rock being so rotted that it frequently gave way. In some hours' work we were able to take all the baggage, partly by passing it down with ropes from one man to another, stationed at various heights upon the rocky wall. Even ourselves had to be let down one by one with ropes in many places where the rock was so smooth and vertical that it was impossible to cling to it; but otherwise we were not roped together, the ropes used being merely those for slinging the loads on the men's backs.

There rose a cutting wind, which made matters even more unpleasant, and drove the sleet and snow with great force into our faces. When the difficult part of the descent was over, and we gradually got lower down, the weather cleared somewhat, and we obtained a good view of the scenery to the north. The vertical rock we had descended measured 600 feet in height.

A magnificent undulating sea of clouds lay before us, screening the lower section of the valley; then three distinct glaciers showed themselves to the north of us, in terraces like gigantic stairways, but with their base hidden in the mist, and barren, desolate, snow-capped mountains rising above them. Then two more glaciers appeared. Above the most northerly of the three glaciers rose a peak 20,279 feet high. As a matter of fact, when the mist cleared up a little more, we discovered that these five glaciers were only the ramifications of one huge glacier, but they were distinctly separated in their upper portion by ridges.

ERECTING CHOKDENS (CAIRNS) ON THE SAVAGE PASS

Several men were taken with mountain sickness.

A sea of clouds is always an interesting sight, annoying as it is, at the time, when it screens the scenery one would like to see. In fact, the formation of clouds upon mountains is altogether an engrossing subject to an observant traveller. The clouds at elevations above the perpetual snow-line (about 16,000 in the Himahlyas) have a more feathery appearance than those formed below, and the higher the elevation the more feathery and light they seem to be. On the snow-line itself one generally saw clouds, chiefly of a globular character, and in such close succession as to form long horizontal streaks. This was particularly noticeable at sunrise and at sunset. During the night, except in case of storms, clouds formed less profusely, and, when they did, disappeared quicker than in the daytime. Just before sunrise, however, when the atmosphere was gradually getting warmer, at elevations from 13,000 to 16,000 feet, mists were constant, which eventually dispersed when the sun was high on the horizon. Towards sunset and soon afterwards they generally recurred again, but the nights were usually very clear. In that particular expedition, being always at very high elevations, I had an opportunity of seeing many phenomena of curious interest and beauty.

One afternoon when I had climbed with two men on a small peak to reconnoitre the country around, we were confronted by a sea of mist down below. The sun was rather low behind us, and it projected our shadows, well defined but in an elongated form of some hundreds of feet, on the sheet of pure white mist beyond. It had quite a weird effect, when we were gesticulating, to see our movements magnified in the shadows to such gigantic proportions.

Another beautiful effect I observed on several occasions when enveloped in mist, of immense white concentric circles with a luminous centre, caused by the sun penetrating through different layers of mist. When under similar circumstances the sun was behind the spectator instead of in front, and the spectator himself not enveloped in the mist, a huge spectre—the spectator's shadow—was often reflected in the centre of the luminous circle. As I have elsewhere described, the latter phenomenon can be produced by the moon or the sun, by the former in a less intensified form, by the latter with a circular rainbow of beautiful colours.

There are many kinds of "seas of mist" upon mountains, some with islands (mountain tops peeping through), some without; some smooth-surfaced

NIGHT MARCHING IN A STORM

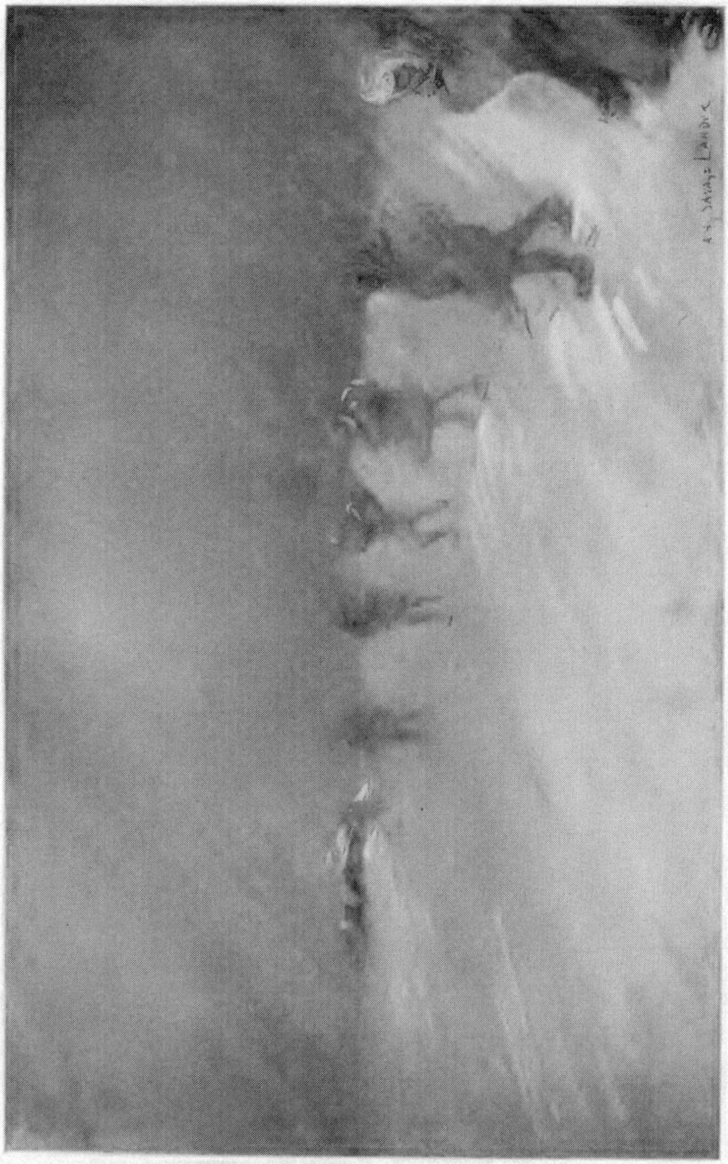

like a placid lake, others in undulations or actual waves like a stormy sea. The shadows and lights play upon the mist and produce many quaint effects, and objects assume curious and interesting shapes.

One misty evening, near the Nui Glacier, I saw before me what seemed an immense crouching lion carved in the rock, not unlike one of the famous lions in Trafalgar Square, only some thousand times bigger. Sure enough you could see the eyes, the luxuriant mane, the extended forepaws, and the tail spread out with the typical end tuft of hair. It was only on getting quite close that the huge animal showed itself to be a mere big boulder, with three *mani* walls with terminal *chokdens* (cairns) erected by Tibetans from its base, which from a distance formed the lion's legs and tail.

So much for optical illusions; there are a thousand more upon high mountains, and it is the number of surprises one meets at every moment which makes a lonely life at great elevations full of enchantment.

Having, on our descent from the Savage Pass, reached a lower elevation and less perilous ground to tread upon, we directed our steps towards 20° (N.E.) bearings magnetic. At 16,100 feet we found moss, but now dead and dry. Unfortunately for us we were benighted before we could find a suitable camping-ground, and a violent snowstorm broke out which made it very difficult to see where we were going. We were endeavouring to get lower down, where we could obtain some shelter and a slightly warmer temperature, my men being simply paralysed with cold. They stumbled along, a row of black silent figures, I keeping the direction in which I wanted to travel with a luminous compass.

We went on for a considerable portion of the night, the storm getting so bad that we could not see where we were putting our feet; and towards midnight, having come across a lot of big boulders, we decided to take advantage of them and make camp. My men were so tired and frozen that they simply threw themselves down, covered themselves up, and went fast asleep, declining to eat any food. They had eaten nothing that day, for they maintained that if you eat food when you are so cold you will surely die. Of course their philosophy does not go quite so far as to reflect whether it is preferable to die of indigestion or from the low temperature. Personally, as I have never been troubled with the former, I thought I would not risk

A SEA OF MIST

the latter. While everybody around snored and moaned or was delirious from pain, I got out a small spirit Etna and attempted to brew myself some hot chocolate. Box after box of matches went in trying to keep it alight, and when, after using the patience of a saint, I had succeeded in making the water tepid, my tent was blown down on the top of us, and upset the whole thing. So, cold chocolate I ate in chunks and some corned beef—oh, it was cold!—and some biscuits.

It was as lonely a meal as I have ever had, with the wind hissing and the snow accumulating upon my shoulders, knees, and head. I did not like to rouse my poor men to put up the tent again, for it was no use, the snow was too deep and the pegs would not hold; but I made myself a sort of low shelter with some boxes and the tent spread on them, and having crept underneath, slept soundly till the morning.

"Oh, what a morning!" I exclaimed, when I opened my aching, half-frozen eyelids. Worse than the night before, and the snow coming down as I have seldom seen it come before. My baggage was buried altogether, and so were my men, except for some breathing-space cleared near the head.

All the urging in the world would not get them up, and every time I gave them a dig in sensitive spots with my bamboo stick, it only brought forth pitiable moans and groans.

Towards 10 A.M. the storm abated somewhat, and we dug out the loads and departed, my men still declining to eat any food. Hungry and shivering, they were indeed a pitiable sight. Their normal sense of humour was sadly lacking that day, and they strode unsteadily, with long, mournful faces, as if they were about to mount the executioner's scaffold.

We went on the whole day mostly in mist and sleet and snow, and towards evening we arrived at the bottom of the valley. Excitement did not altogether lack. Three avalanches came down during the day with deafening *fracas.* One of them, which brought down a lot of *débris* and rock, sounded like a regular battle, with sharp fusilading and big artillery, with a deafening report at the end which almost stunned us.

Next we came to a broad river which it was necessary to ford, and wading across it chilled us about as much as we could endure. Our toes got so cold—almost frost-bitten—that it required some minutes of rubbing and thumping before we could

ELONGATED SHADOWS ON A SEA OF MIST

stand upon them again. The pain was quite excruciating.

While we were in this plight we heard voices. We answered, and presently two Jumli shepherds, half-scared and shaggy, cautiously approached us. We received the information that some few more hours' marching would take us to the village of Tinker, and for it we made with renewed vigour. Stumbling and slipping constantly after it got dark, we went on and on. More snow, more wind. Hour after hour passed, but no village. At last, at 3 A.M., my men half-dead with fatigue and hunger, we arrived at the modest little village of Tinker. My men had wilfully been forty consecutive hours without a morsel of food, but once under a roof with a blazing fire, they were now preparing to make up for lost time.

CHAPTER XI

TINKER is a village of Shokas, at no less an elevation by hypsometrical apparatus than 12,664 feet. Our arrival necessarily caused a great deal of commotion, and everybody was up to see what was happening.

It is the custom in that part of Nepal—a habit of all Shokas generally—that no stranger must enter a village after sunset without sending a messenger ahead to warn the residents; so, according to their code of manners, we were committing a gross breach of etiquette. I well knew this, and upon arrival immediately asked for the chieftain of the village to express my sorrow that we were unable to advise him of our arrival.

The chief was a splendid fellow—an old friend of mine—a man with a heart of gold and the manner of a most polished gentleman. He placed his house at my disposal, and showered upon us

CONCENTRIC CIRCLES OF RADIANT
BEAUTY FORMED BY THE SUN
SHINING THROUGH MIST

lavish presents of food—fresh meat, rice, *ghiúr*, and dried fruit. He would on no account accept money, so I gave him presents of various kinds, and distributed the money among his family and servants.

I have ever made it a rule never to accept presents from anybody anywhere, and, when gifts are forced upon me, to give back some gift of equivalent value. With natives particularly I ever followed this golden rule, nevertheless displaying gratitude for their thoughtful offerings.

The house in which we dwelt was a stone structure, the rooms only some 7 feet high, with little slits of windows and a somewhat disjointed door. When a huge fire was lighted in the room, with no escape for the smoke or heat, you were simply roasted and suffocated, but after our cold, fireless nights on the glaciers this felt to us the most comfortable and luxurious abode we had ever been in. Fleas there were in abundance—little fleas with marvellous jumping powers, and giant ones of astounding voracity. With their proverbial partiality for strangers, they of course directed their undivided attention to us new-comers, and particularly to me. In a moment we were covered with hundreds of bites.

The chieftain told me how the Tibetans on the frontier close by were in a great state of excitement over my approach. They boasted of having 5000 soldiers ready to meet me, and hearing that I was now on Nepal territory they had despatched them to the Tinker Pass to capture me. The Tibetans had been for some days busy polishing up their matchlocks and grinding their swords, and they had accumulated large piles of stones to precipitate down upon me in ravines which we had to get through. The same stories I had on many occasions heard before, both on my previous journey into Tibet and on the present.

When we got up in the morning a great many yaks came in laden with Tibetan wool, which the natives barter with Tibetans in exchange for foodstuff, and also long strings of sheep and goats with double sacks slung across the back and filled with borax. With some of these caravans, unluckily, arrived—unseen by me—some Tibetan spies, and they at once set to work to scare the villagers. There was a sudden commotion in the village, the natives ran here and there conveying their children, goods, and chattels into their houses, and in these they barricaded themselves. Only the chief remained cool and collected; and, to avoid getting

CLOUDS FORMING ON THE SNOW-LINE

him into trouble, and by way of precaution, I shifted my quarters from his house to a high point commanding the village, where I pitched my tents, placing men with loaded rifles on guard of my baggage.

It looked very much as if there were trouble brewing ahead. Some of these Nepalese Shokas are very curious people, shifty and unfathomable, the life they lead being one of semi-brigandage and trading. They are interesting enough as a type—flat-faced and of strongly Mongolian features, as in the portraits of the long-haired young men I give in two of the coloured plates—and they have from contact adopted some of the dash and independence of the Nepalese. We took no notice of the warlike preparations, and when some young fellows, bolder than the rest, came out of their houses to inform us rudely that we must go at once, they duly had their heads punched. We would go when it pleased me, and not before.

Bad luck never comes singly, but it can sometimes be turned into good luck. A Nepalese agent also arrived early that morning, and could persuade no more messengers to come and approach me on the subject of departing from their country, so he had to come on the errand himself.

With many salaams the Nepalese officer came forth, and, after tender inquiries after every possible existing and imaginary relative of mine he could think of, he gently entered upon the question of my leaving the country. Asked whether he would like his head punched too, or a gift of five rupees not to worry me and induce the natives to sell me 300 lbs. of rice, some goats, *ghur*, and butter, he at once said he preferred the five rupees, and would endeavour to do all he could to be of assistance. In fact, he went into the village again, and shortly after the provisions were duly sold to me.

You see, five rupees would be to him, in Nepal, as much as he would receive in cash from his Government for two months' salary.

We sacrificed a goat for luck—the luck consisting chiefly in the dinner that followed—and in the afternoon we made a start in order to cross the Tibetan frontier.

The Tinker village is perched on a height some distance from the spot where the two principal sources of the Tinker river join—one coming from the five glaciers to the east (those described in the previous chapter), the other source descending precipitously and with great force from the Tinker

AUTHOR'S TENTS. A CAMP IN NEPAL

A. H. Savage Landor

Glacier higher up, to the north of the village, and spreading in a N.E. direction.

Tinker itself is a quaint and interesting place. Flying prayers—generally pieces of white cloth—decorated every roof in the village, and some shrubs were similarly decorated with hundreds of strips of cloth—red, blue, or white—deposited there by devotees. *Chokdens*—piles of stones—were numerous, many of them constructed of stones each of which was inscribed with the Tibetan prayer—"*Omni mani padme hun.*"

Farther up the mountain one found curious ancient cave-dwellings, identical with those I have in a previous work described at Taklakot, in Tibet, the peculiar composition of the rock permitting the chambers to be hollowed out with comparative ease. These dwellings are very suitable for that climate, being relatively warm in winter and cool in summer, besides answering all the purposes of a fortress when built high up into a cliff. In Tibet itself these cliff-dwellings are most elaborate, and are connected by means of intricate passages and galleries going right up to the summit of the high cliff. Outer ways of communication are also noticeable, in the form of dangerous-looking steps and sharp and narrow gradients, by which the lodgers can find access to or escape from their apartments.

Upon the higher Himahlyas, in certain selected points, such as on passes, or where two trails branch off, or near villages, is generally to be found a gay exhibition of flying prayers, hundreds of them, suspended from ropes stretched across upon high poles. Large banners are also frequently to be seen at these spots. Passing caravans make these favourite halting-places. Both the women of Tibet and those of neighbouring tribes often select these spots for stretching their hand-looms and weaving their fabrics.

The Tinker Glacier was a very beautiful sight with its high terraces, and we followed it for its entire length on our way up to the pass. It was a long and steep climb, mostly on snow, and as the trail was low down between high mountains to the S.W. and N.E. the sun did not penetrate for any length of time, so that the cold was intense. My men were rather heavily laden, and at sunset, owing to our late start, we had gone but a few miles.

We halted at a Tibetan camping-ground, where there were a number of black Tibetan tents, their occupants bolting full-speed up the mountain-side as soon as they saw us. After some coaxing, and promises that we would in no way harm them, they gradually returned and attended to their business. The women had erected a great many looms outside the tents, and some jolly, but somewhat shaggy, females were noisily and busily engaged beating wool previous to packing; others were spinning it and winding it round long rods; others were speedily making narrow strips of cloth upon their looms. Upon receiving small presents they became quite friendly, and gave much information regarding the war preparations of their countrymen. They said thousands of soldiers were guarding the pass.

Next morning I went to see for myself, but the Tibetan soldiers had, when I arrived, already beaten a hasty retreat, leaving nothing more than their footmarks on the snow. Although I constantly heard of this formidable army, I never was able to catch it up during my incursions, or establish its exact position, much less meet it.

Everybody has heard so much of late of Tibetan scenery and travelling that it will perhaps be more agreeable to the reader if I devote most of the space which remains at my disposal to the description of some Tibetan customs. It is well known that Tibet is a high plateau, S.W. Tibet especially, where most of my exploration extended, averaging heights of from 15,000 to 19,000 feet, so that people who live in such a climate and such a country are bound to have peculiarities of their own, and their ways offer many curious problems.

First of all, I will answer some of the most common questions—generally very stupid—which I am daily being asked by people who try to be clever, about the Forbidden Land.

"If you say that Tibet is such a high plateau, barren and cold, with no trees and no agriculture to speak of, how is it that the people live there?"

Well, if people stop to think a little, the same question applies to every country. Why do negroes live in Central Africa, where it is so hot? Why do people go and live in Panama, where it is so unhealthy? Why do we live in London, where it is so foggy and damp? In the case of the Tibetans, as with everybody else in regard to their native land, they believe that no country in the world can possibly compare with their own — which, indeed, in a sense, is true. They believe their land is the most beautiful, the richest, the healthiest on earth, their religion the only one, their civilisation the highest.

The Tibetans, having lived for so many generations at such great altitudes, suffer a great deal

THE TINKER PASS, NEPAL-TIBET

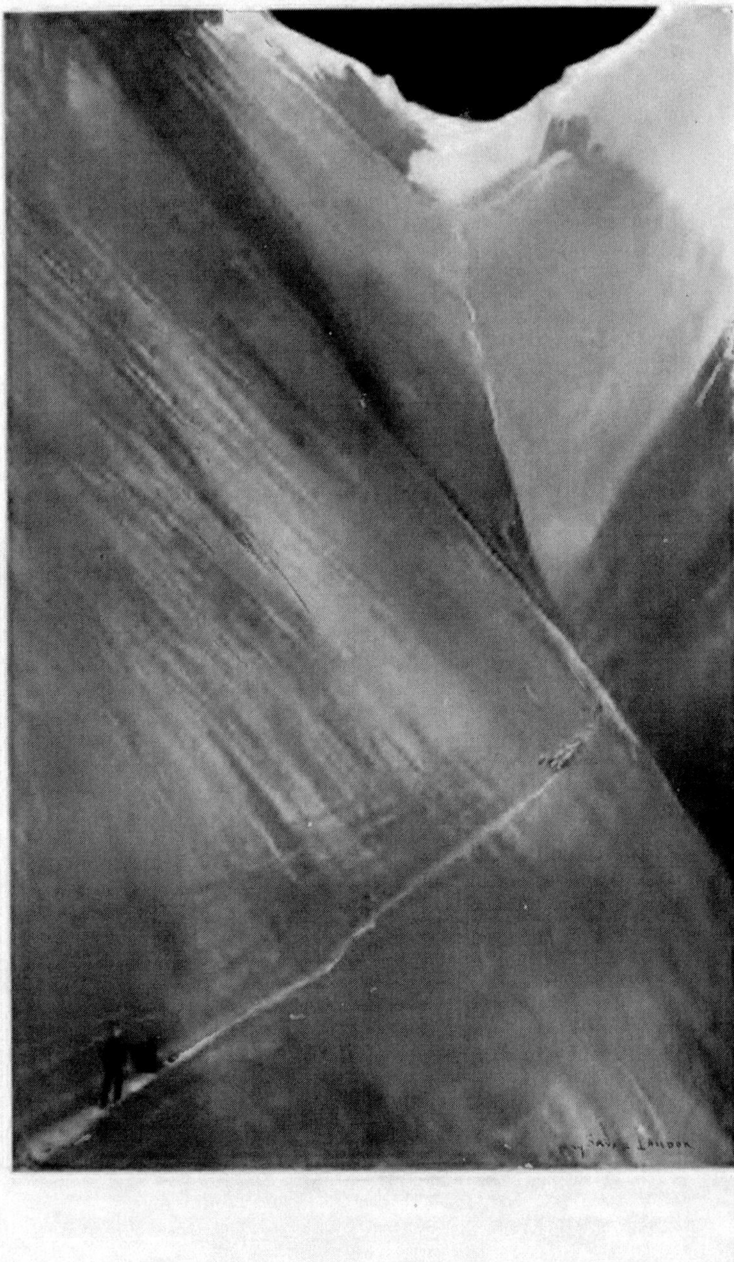

when they travel to lower elevations, and they experience a feeling of suffocation and heaviness which makes them very ill and frequently causes their death. This is not so much the case with natives of the Sikkim district and of Lhassa, which are at a much lower elevation; but I am talking principally of the natives of S.W. Tibet, few of whom live at an elevation of less than 15,000 feet.

"Then," say other wise folks, "if you maintain that next to nothing grows in Tibet, that the people are not farmers, how do they manage to live?"

The answer is simple. The Tibetans import all their food from India, Nepal, Cashmere, and China during the summer months, while the snow-passes are open, and they store it in sufficient quantities to last them all through the winter. Wheat, rice, *tsamba* (a kind of oatmeal), *ghur* (sweet paste), sugar are bartered in large quantities in exchange for borax, salt, sheep, and yak wool.

Another question that seems to puzzle most people is why polyandry exists legally in Tibet instead of our marriage customs or polygamy, and in the next chapter I will endeavour to explain the reason, as well as why women are so much less numerous than men.

CHAPTER XII

THE first two things that strike an observant traveller on entering a Tibetan encampment are that the number of children in the population is so small, and that the majority of Tibetans appear, to European eyes, middle-aged, or even old and decrepit. The second remark is more easily explained than the first, and many are the reasons which cause Tibetan men and women to look well on in years long before they have attained a really advanced age. I have seen a man with hands and face so wrinkled that he might easily pass for an octogenarian, yet he was no more than three-and-forty.

The women manage to preserve their complexion slightly better than the men, by smearing the cheeks, nose, and forehead with a black ointment. This, to a certain extent, prevents the skin chapping in the cold, but the winds in Tibet are so terrific that

FLYING PRAYERS AND A MANI WALL

The wall is constructed of stones, on each of which is inscribed a prayer. In the foreground a woman is weaving on one of the small portable looms.

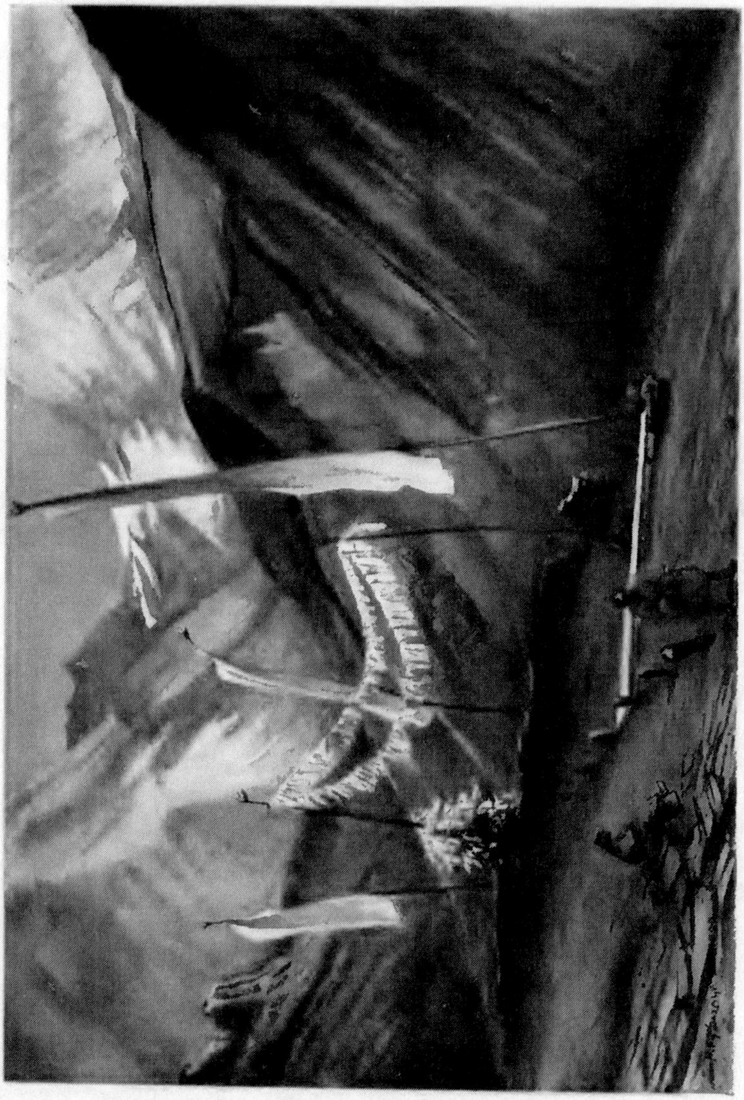

they are disastrous to any human skin, whether besmeared with grease or not. Indeed, no one who has not been in Tibet knows what wind can be. I cannot better describe a gale than by likening it to myriads of knives thrown at one with great force. It cuts into one through any kind of clothing, and penetrates to the marrow of one's bones. The skin, particularly where exposed, chaps and cracks and becomes a mass of sores, unless the constant precaution is taken of keeping it well soaked in butter, grease, or vaseline.

Again, the intense glare of the snow-covered landscape and the extraordinary brilliancy of the atmosphere compel the natives constantly to frown—as may be noticed in many of the illustrations reproduced in this work—in order to screen their semi-closed eyes as much as possible from the blinding light. This everlasting frown, of course, covers the forehead with deep wrinkles and grooves, while "crow's feet" in continuation of the outward corners of the eyes and deep channels at both ends of the lips disfigure the faces of Tibetans at an early age. Naturally, to a European these wrinkles at once suggest age, whereas they are merely caused by the inclement weather, and they have been the chief cause which has led casual observers to describe the population of Tibet as composed mainly of old people.

Another curious fact worth noticing is that, according to theoretical scientists, the greatly rarefied air of the Tibetan plateau should retard the growth of human beings, and that therefore a Tibetan should reach the age of puberty later in life than people living in a corresponding latitude but at lower elevations. This is not the case at all. Tibetan boys and girls attain a state of maturity at a comparatively early age. I have often noticed girls of fifteen or sixteen and boys of eighteen or nineteen fully developed, and it is at these respective ages that men and women of Tibet frequently marry.

Now let us try to explain why one sees so few children in Tibet. Personally, I think it is mainly due to the custom of polyandry prevailing in the country, which is bound to have disastrous effects upon the birth-rate of healthy, strong children, with deteriorating results upon every generation; and also undoubtedly the altitudes at which the people live to a great extent limit the increase of population. The generally unhealthy condition of most Tibetans' blood also greatly contributes to the non-fertility of parents.

TIBETAN BABY GIRL

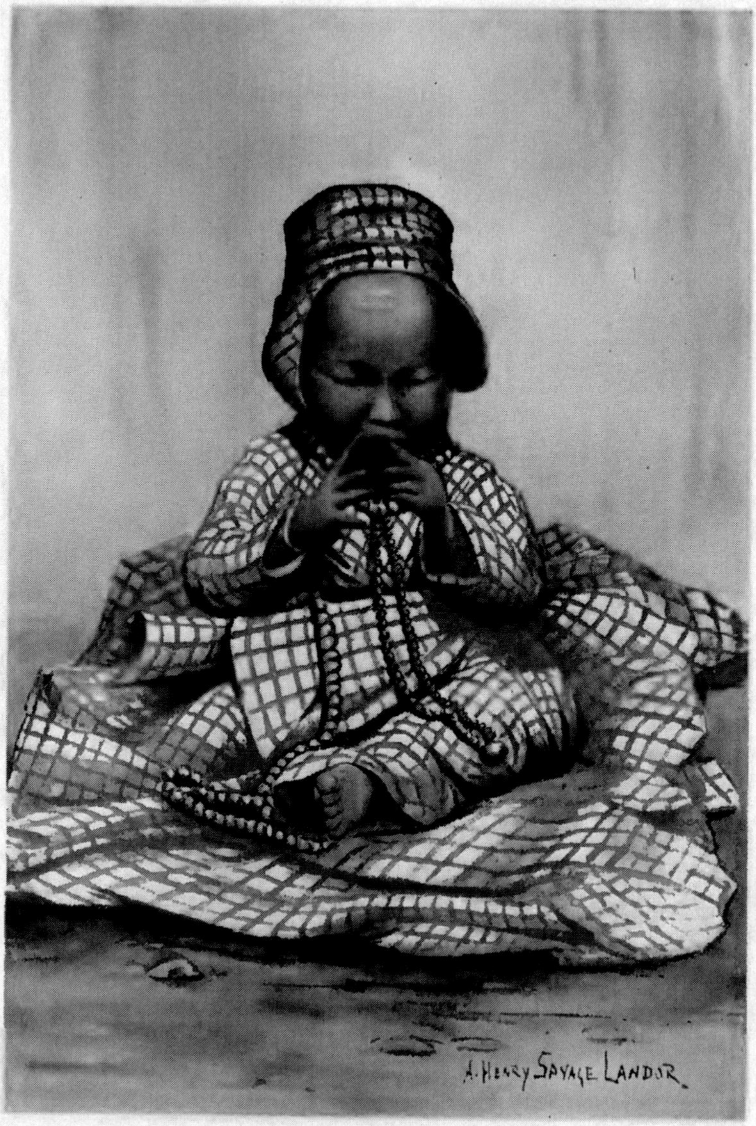
A. HENRY SAVAGE LANDOR

We have yet another curious fact. To an average of fifteen male children who are born and live in Tibet, only one female child is healthy enough to survive. There are various reasons for this, and it would be difficult to discover the primary one; but in my mind, and from personal observation, I could not help associating that fact with these two principal causes. First, the food diet of the parents, which certainly has marked effects on the production of one sex more than another; secondly, the greater mortality among the weaker female children. Tibetans always told me that the death-rate in children under the age of two years was very great in proportion to the number of births.

It is impossible to give exact statistics, but, from constant inquiry from families I met, I came to the conclusion that an average of three children out of seven born succumb before the age of five. Of these deaths, the majority would be female children.

The life of a Tibetan baby is not a merry one at best. He is cherished by his mother when newly born, and for some days the new-comer affords amusement to the tent-mates and the members of the tribe. Occasional caresses are bestowed upon him, but the trials of having a loving mother soon begin. She will besmear him from head to foot several times daily with yak butter, the mother realising that by this process the skin of her infant will be made impervious to cold; and with maternal fondness she will press and force the butter into every pore of his little body. This done, the baby is left naked in the sun so that under the heat of its rays his skin may absorb the maximum of melted butter.

His next torture comes in the shape of piercing his poor little ears. The lobes are rubbed between the first finger and thumb until they become numbed, then with a long silver or brass pin the hole is made, the fond mother being again the operator. As care is never taken to disinfect the pin from the accumulation of dirt upon it, and as that very same pin has for generations been used in the various capacities of tooth-, nose-, and ear-pick, nail-cleaner, and head- and back-scratcher, it is not infrequent to find that the ear-piercing operation is accompanied by inflammation or some nasty sore or other, causing the little fellow much unnecessary pain. Heavy ear-rings are next inserted, elongating and disfiguring the little ears, in many instances the

A TIBETAN GIRL

A. H. Savage Landor

lobes actually tearing down altogether owing to the weight of the ear-ring.

Until a few months old the baby is made to lie in a basket, in which he is carried about on his mother's back—that is to say, if the mother is in a comfortable enough position to own a basket. Otherwise she will carry him on her back, suspended by his little arms, which she tightly clasps over her shoulders; and as this mode of transport somewhat lacks comfort, it is rather curious to notice the intelligence of Tibetan babies in order to feel the least inconvenience possible. Under similar circumstances the average civilised baby who felt his little arms almost pulled out of their sockets would very likely cry and scream, helplessly dangling his legs in order to be again deposited on *terra firma.* The Tibetan baby knows better. Guided only by his instincts, he will clasp his mother's waist with his little toes, so supple that he can use them almost like fingers. By thus supporting his own weight upon her hips in the identical position of a monkey climbing a tree, the tension on his arms is absolutely released and he looks quite at his ease, even comfortable.

Babies in Tibet, as in other lands, do not lack a temporary charm. They are by nature good, well-behaved babies; occasionally they are even jolly. The clothes in which their mothers garb them are not devoid of quaintness,—as can be judged by some of the illustrations,—and if often size is preferred to style, it is, as in most countries, for economy's sake. Sometimes I have seen babies simply smothered in beads and ornaments, but even the humblest displays a row of beads round his neck and a charm or two.

Notwithstanding what has been said of the strange marital customs, the average Tibetan woman is seldom absolutely sterile. This, of course, is mainly due to the fact that if she survives at all to the age of puberty, it is because she is strong and healthy; but at best she is never so prolific as her Asiatic sisters or even European women. In Tibet one rarely finds a woman with more than three living children. The majority of mothers can only boast of one. Yet, on the other hand, the Tibetan woman can bear children until a fairly advanced age. I remember meeting a lady who acknowledged her age—after complicated computation with the aid of fingers and toes—to be forty. Her skin was so wrinkled and rough that without maliciousness one could have put her down at fifty-five, but maybe she spoke the truth

TIBETAN WOMAN OF THE COMMONER CLASS

A.H. SAVAGE LANDOR

—she certainly was not less than what she had stated. She carried in her arms a baby a few months old.

"It is my baby," she proudly said, screening with her hand the fat offspring to prevent the "evil eye" of an inquisitive foreigner. "Go away; do not touch him or he will die."

I was in a chaffing mood, and chaff in Tibet can never be too personal.

"I do not believe that he can be your baby, for he has a smooth skin and yours is rough and wrinkled. Were he your child he would have a skin like yours."

The woman, half-amused, half-astonished, called witnesses to testify that the baby was really hers, and after assumed reluctance I acknowledged that there existed some resemblance between mother and son, in the lack of nose.

"Why," I asked her, "did you not have the child sooner, so that he might now be a help and comfort to you in your old age?"

She said she had had two other children, but they had died, one when only "a few moons" old, the other when about four years of age.

With the exception of the few larger towns, Tibet is peopled by small, semi-nomadic tribes. A large tribe may number a hundred tents, but the average is from ten to fifty tents. Each tent is inhabited by one family, although investigation generally brings out the fact that nearly all members of a tribe are related to one another owing to the constant intermarriage among themselves.

This constant intermarriage also contributes to a great extent to the decadence of the race generally, and to the diminution of the population with each generation.

I had several opportunities of noticing the difference which existed when either the wife or husband had come from a distant tribe. There were generally more children to the union, and they were invariably stronger, both physically and mentally. The Tibetans are well aware of this, and when a tribe is likely to die out from the causes I have stated, fresh blood is imported into it by the advice of the Lamas in order to revive it.

I found that the cleverer men I met in the country were generally born from parents of different tribes, and not infrequently of widely separated social positions.

In cases of crosses between different races altogether, such as a Tibetan and a Nepalese, for

TIBETAN LADY

instance, or a Shoka, or other frontier tribes, the families were larger; but these semi-foreign marriages are not common, and cannot be given as a general rule.

Wilful infanticide is seldom practised in Tibet, and cannot be put down as one of the causes limiting population. It, of course, occasionally occurs, for instance, in order to suppress an illegitimate child, but the custom is greatly looked down upon by Tibetans, although no punishment—beyond the contempt of the entire tribe—would be meted out to the culprits.

The women of Tibet are seldom separated from one or other of their husbands. When one man goes for some days to take the yaks or sheep to a distant grazing ground, another fills his place in the tent. Occasionally more than one of her legal husbands live together happily under the same tent, but usually not more than one at a time.

As I have fully explained in a previous book, *In the Forbidden Land*, marriages are principally family arrangements, where a girl becomes the wife of several brothers; and, in any case, bachelors are, as a whole, to be greatly congratulated in Tibet.

Other minor causes there are which tend to

limit population, but which cannot very well be mentioned here. Several diseases of the blood—very common—decidedly do not improve the race; and possibly all these evils—some natural, some unnatural—may in time bring about the disappearance of the Tibetan race from their lofty and sacred land.

AN OLD LADY AND HER PRAYER WHEEL

A. HENRY SAVAGE LANDOR

CHAPTER XIII

ANOTHER thing that strikes the traveller in Tibet is the sturdiness of Tibetan ponies,—long-haired, short, stumpy little brutes, which possess most marvellous endurance under circumstances which would kill most horses. They live on whatever grass they can find, which is not much—at best, short semi-dried blades which take a good deal of looking for before you can see them at all. Tibet ponies have all the qualities of a goat and antelope combined, and I have seen them, with a rider on their back, go up gradients where a human being would have great difficulty to go up on foot.

The dogs of Tibet are not quite so attractive, being either vicious to a degree or else stupid, lazy, and uninteresting. The common kind is not unlike our sheep-dog, except that the hair is longer, which in some cases gives them a slight appearance of collie dogs. They are generally ill-treated and suffering, and they seem to have no affection for anybody. They possess plenty of intelligence, especially those trained by shepherds, and they are indeed a great help to their masters in driving the flock in the right direction and keeping the sheep together. These sheep-dogs are generally made to carry a broad leather collar with an immense brass bell.

Perhaps, talking of dogs' affection, I might here give some account of a Tibetan dog—a friend of mine—that I met on my first expedition into Tibet, while I was being chased all over the country by the Tibetan army. One night, during a storm, we were attacked, and I heard a number of voices around my camp. I only had two men left, and we jumped up to defend ourselves. Stones were flung at us with slings—an art at which both Tibetan men and women excel. From their earliest childhood they keep in constant practice at flinging stones, and in daylight they can hit the mark with great accuracy. Shepherds use them constantly, and can pick out any sheep in a flock of hundreds. We kept close to the ground, rifle in hand, a few feet from our tent, to avoid being hit, as evidently they were aiming at it, it being of a lightish colour. They struck it several times. With them was a

TIBETAN DOGS

dog barking furiously all the time. Dog and men seemed to be approaching—at least, by the sounds of their voices, for I could not see them. This seemed an appropriate time to fire a shot, which would undoubtedly, as usual, cause a stampede. It did. Only the dog remained, barking and yelping the whole night, but we were otherwise not troubled in any other way, although, of course, we kept watch until sunrise, when all we found were numerous fresh footmarks a few yards from our tent.

The dog ran about a good deal, barking and barking, until we prepared our breakfast, when he sat himself down upon his hindquarters and watched the proceedings with keen interest. He seemed very shy, and whenever we tried to get near him he bolted away with his tail between his legs, howling madly as if he had been hit by a stone. Dogs in Tibet are so accustomed to have stones flung at them at every possible opportunity that no doubt in his imagination he fancied he had been hit by a missile each time we raised our hand to caress him. Animals are not unlike people in that way.

At last, by offers of tinned meat and the use of the favourite Tibetan term of endearment,

"Chochu, chochu," the dog became our friend. He seemed utterly astonished at being caressed, and rubbed himself affectionately against our legs. He took a particular fancy to Mansing, my faithful man who developed leprosy, and from that day the dog followed us everywhere. Mansing, who was suffering considerably, and who took no interest whatever in scientific observations, photography, surveying, etc., had at last a sympathising friend to whom he could confide his grievances. The two were inseparable, and whenever we stopped Mansing pathetically conversed with the dog, who seemed almost to understand all the coolie was telling him.

It was rather a puzzle to me why this dog followed us so long, for we had so little food that we could but seldom spare him any. He slept near us at night with his head on the lap of one of us, and during the march he showed quite sporting instincts by chasing antelopes and *kiang* (wild horse) when we encountered herds of hundreds of them. Curiously enough, when we entered a Tibetan encampment he always avoided being seen in our company. It seemed almost as if he realised that we were not welcome guests in the country, and feared the consequences. Possibly

A TIBETAN CAMP OF BLACK TENTS

he only temporarily left us to see what he could pick up in the way of food, but whenever we came across him in the encampment, he never would show signs of recognition, much less of affection, as was the case when he would rejoin us some miles beyond on the march, when he made ample efforts to reingratiate himself. He seemed almost to want to express: "Sorry I had to cut you in the encampment, but I really had to!"

At last the day came when we were captured, and underwent several kinds of tortures, as I have already described in *In the Forbidden Land.* The dog had vanished, and, to tell the truth, we did not give him much of a thought, as we were somewhat concerned about ourselves.

One day, when Mansing and I were stretched, or rather suspended, on a primitive kind of rack, and we were for some time left to ourselves—the soldiers and Lamas having retired some distance off into the huge tent of the Pombo, a high official—the dog sadly walked towards us, sniffing us, and rubbing himself against Mansing and me. He was particularly affectionate to Mansing, whose face he licked several times; then with a pathetic movement of his head as if to express his sorrow, he gave us a parting sad look, turned his back, and walked slowly and sorrowfully away. That was his last mark of friendship and the last we saw of him.

Tibetan encampments have no great interest except for the peculiar shape of the black tents—a pattern of shelter most suitable for the climate of their country. The two sides of the tent are separate, and when the tent is put up it leaves an aperture all along its highest ridge. This is for various reasons. First, because the Tibetans light fires inside their tents, and an opening is necessary to let the smoke out; also as a means of ventilation, the cold air not penetrating so quickly as when it comes in at the sides, owing to the warmed atmosphere inside. The black tents are woven of a coarse and waterproof fabric of yak hair. Through the slit at the top generally protrude the props of the matchlocks bundled against one of the tent poles.

Every man in Tibet owns one of these weapons, and is considered a soldier in time of war.

The inside of a large Tibetan tent is quaint enough when you have reached it by skipping over masses of dirt and refuse which surround its outside. Only, when you peep in, the odour is rather strong of the people, old and young, all since

INTERIOR OF A TIBETAN TENT,
SHOWING CHURN FOR MIXING TEA
WITH BUTTER

birth innocent of washing, and the smell of badly-prepared skins, and stores of *chura* (cheese). Nor must I forget to mention the wall of yak-dung erected right round the tent inside to serve the double purpose of protection against the wind where the tent meets the ground, and of fuel, being gradually demolished to feed the double mud-stove erected in the centre of the tent. Mud alone is also occasionally used for the inside wall.

As you know, dung is practically the only fuel obtainable in the highest parts of Tibet, although occasionally a few low shrubs are to be found. The fuel is constantly collected and conveyed from one camp to the next, when changing in order to find more suitable grazing for the sheep and yaks.

The centre mud-stove is built according to the most practical notions to make it draw properly, and upon it can nearly always be seen one or two large *raksangs*, brass vessels in which brick-tea is being stewed and stirred with a long brass spoon. But the operation of tea-making is rather complicated in Tibet. After the leaves have been stewed long enough the liquid is poured into a *dongbo*, or cylindrical wooden churn, in which have been deposited several balls of butter with copious sprinkling of salt. A piston which passes through the movable lid is then vigorously set in action, and when well stirred and steaming the mixture is served all round and avidly drunk in wooden bowls, one of which every one carries about the person. *Tsamba*, a kind of oatmeal, is frequently mixed with the tea in the bowls, where it is made into a paste with the fingers.

No matter how much non-Tibetan folks may find merriment in the idea of tea being brewed with butter and salt, there is no doubt that for a climate like Tibet it is "the drink" *par excellence.* It warms, nourishes, and is easily digested. I very often indulged in the luxury myself, when I could obtain butter, only, my digestion working rather rapidly owing to the amount of roughing we daily endured, I left out the salt so that I should not digest the mixture too quickly.

The richer owners of tents generally have a sort of folding shrine, with one or more images of Buddha, which occupies the place of honour in the tent. Numerous brass bowls and ornaments are displayed in front of these images and also offerings of *tsamba* and butter. Wicks, burning in butter, are occasionally lighted around and upon the shrine. Decrepit old women seem to

A LITTLE BOY LEARNING TO PRAY

A. HENRY SAVAGE LANDOR

spend most of their time revolving their prayer-wheels and muttering prayers in front of these altars, and when occasion arises thus teaching little children to do the same. The younger folk, too, are very religious, but not to the fanatical extent of the older ones.

It is quite amusing to see little mites—children are always quaint in every country—try to master the art of revolving the prayer-wheel. It must be revolved from left to right, to pray in the proper fashion,—not that if you revolved it the other way you would necessarily be swearing, only, according to the laws of Tibetan Buddhism, prayers spun in the wrong direction would have no effect and bring no benefit. In a similar way circumambulations, either round hills for pilgrimages, or round a tent, or round a sacred lake, must always follow a similar direction to the revolving of the prayer-wheel.

In Lhassa and many other sacred places fanatical pilgrims make these circumambulations, sometimes for miles and miles, and for days together, covering the entire distance lying flat upon their bodies, then placing the feet where the head was and stretching themselves full length. Inside temples a central enclosure is provided, round which these circumambulations are performed, special devotions being offered before Buddha and many of the other gilt or high-coloured images which adorn the walls of the temple.

As can be seen by the coloured plate illustrating one of these scenes, from the ceiling of the temple hang hundreds of long strips, *Katas,* offered by pilgrims to the temple and becoming so many flying prayers when hung up—for mechanical praying in every way is prominent in Tibet. There is, after all, no reason why praying should not be made easy like everything else. Thus, instead of having to learn by heart long and varied prayers, all you have to do is to stuff the entire prayer-book (written on a roll in Tibet) into the prayer-wheel, and revolve it while repeating as fast as you can go these four words: "*Omni mani padme hun,*"—words of Sanscrit origin and referring to the reincarnation of Buddha from a lotus flower, literally "O God, the gem emerging from the lotus flower."

The temples of Tibet, except in Lhassa itself, are not beautiful in any way—in fact, they are generally very tawdry and dirty. The attention of the pilgrims is directed to a large box, or often a big bowl, where they may deposit whatever

INTERIOR OF TIBETAN TEMPLE

Worshippers circumambulating the inner enclosure lying flat full length.

offerings they can spare, and it must be said that their religious ideas are so strongly developed that they will dispose of a considerable portion of their money in this fashion.

Large monasteries, of red or yellow Lamas, are attached to these temples, where proselytes are also educated. These Lamas, whatever their colour, are very clever in many ways, and have a great hold over the entire country. They are, ninety per cent of them, unscrupulous scamps, depraved in every way, and given to every sort of vice. So are the women Lamas. They live and sponge on the credulity and ignorance of the crowds; and it is to maintain this ignorance, upon which their luxurious life depends, that foreign influence of every kind is strictly kept out of the country. Their abnormal powers have been grossly exaggerated. They practise, it is true, hypnotism, but that is all. They can perform no more marvellous feats than any one can do in England who is able to mesmerize. As for the Mahatmas, who, our spiritualistic friends tell us, live in Tibet, they are purely imaginary, and do not exist. The Tibetans have never heard of them nor about their doings.

Personally—and I am glad that the few men

who know Tibet from personal knowledge and not from political rivalry agree with me—I believe that the intrigues of the Lamas with Russia are absolute nonsense. Tibet, it must be remembered, was not forbidden to Englishmen only, but to everybody from every side, whether native or white, certain Nepalese and Chinamen, only, having the privilege of entering the country. It was a fight against Western ways in general which the Lamas were carrying on, quite successfully owing to the geographical position of their country, and the natural difficulties of reaching it, and not a fight against one race more than another. The accounts of the Lhassa Mission to the Czar were possibly the best diplomatic practical jokes which have been played upon this credulous country; and the mythical and much-feared Dorjeff is possibly—at least as far as power is concerned—nothing more than the creation of hysterical Anglo-Indian officials who, everybody knows, seem to see the treacherous hand of Russia in everything.

Perhaps no other country but England would be so rash as to go and sink millions of pounds sterling good money on a country that is, for all practical purposes, absolutely useless and worthless.

TIBETAN WOMEN WEAVING

This does not detract from its pictorial, nor from its geographical or ethnological interest; from these points it is most interesting indeed.

Agriculturally, as I have stated, nothing grows there; no very wealthy mines have so far been discovered, the only mines that are plentiful being of borax, which has not sufficient market value to pay for the expensive carriage from Tibet to the coast. Regarded as a climate for a sanatorium for our sick soldiers in India—for which Tibet is frequently recommended by Anglo-Indian papers—I believe that such an establishment would be a very quick way of disposing altogether of all the sick men sent there. And as for such gigantic schemes as the construction of railways, say from India to the upper waters of the Yangtze-Kiang, or to Pekin, the expense of taking a railway over the Himahlya range and keeping it in working order during the wintry months—nine out of twelve—would, I think, never be remunerative. In Tibet itself the construction of a railway would be comparatively easy, as great stretches of the country are almost flat. Stations of imported fuel would have to be provided for the entire distance across Tibet, and the engines would have to be constructed specially to suit the great altitude.

For trade and commerce with the natives themselves, the population of the country is so small, so deplorably poor and so lacking in wants, and the country is so large that, personally, I do not see how any large commercial venture in such a country can turn out successful. It is very difficult to get money where there is none. Small native traders, of course, can make small profits and be satisfied. Besides, the intercourse between Tibet and the neighbouring countries, particularly those to the south, can only take place with comfort during three months of the summer when the high snow-passes are open.

So that, much as I would like to see Tibet open in a proper way to travellers, I cannot quite understand the necessity of the Government spending millions of money and butchering thousands of helpless and defenceless natives in a manner most repulsive to any man who is a man, and of which we can but be ashamed—and all this to obtain a valueless commercial treaty. It is true, the Tibetans had been very impudent in every way on our frontier, but for this we only have to blame ourselves and our incompetent officials. If, instead of giving way to their bluff, we had kept a firm hand, matters would have been different.

TIBETAN WOMEN CLEANING WOOL

Even in the case of my capture and torture on my first expedition into Tibet I never had a feeling of resentment towards the Tibetans for what they did to me. It was very exciting and interesting for me to endeavour to reach their sacred city, but I did so at my own risk and against their repeated warnings and threats, and I got nothing more for it in the end than I expected, in fact, bad as it was, considerably less. Highly amusing as it was to me to give them endless trouble, it was undoubtedly equally enjoyable to them to torture me, when once they succeeded in effecting my capture. Possibly, if I now have any feelings at all towards the Tibetans, it is a feeling of gratitude towards them for sparing my life in the end, which, by the way, they came within an ace of taking as they had promised to do.

As a punishment for what they did to me—because, after all, my men and I suffered a great deal more than the average man could stand—the Government of India practically ceded, as we have said, all the rights to Tibet of an immense district of British territory at the frontier. Can you blame the Tibetans for doing worse if they had a chance?

CHAPTER XIV

In heart and soul the Tibetan is a sportsman; but if you look for grace in his movements you will be sorely disappointed. Indeed, more fervour and clumsiness combined are hardly to be paralleled anywhere. Perhaps the Tibetan is seen to advantage on his pony, and some of his feats on the saddle I will here describe.

Horse races are quite a favourite form of amusement, and are run in a sensible manner. Only two ponies at a time go round the course, the final race being run between the winners of the two best heats. Praying is usually combined, in some form or other, with everything people do in Tibet, and so even races are run round the foot of an isolated hill or around an encampment of tents; for, as you know, circumambulation of any kind, if in the right direction, is equivalent to prayer, and pleases God. Thus, just as with their prayer-wheels, a rotatory

A LAMA STANDARD-BEARER

A H SAVAGE LANDOR

motion is kept up from left to right, so races are run in the same way from the standpoint of the spectator.

A Tibetan race would astonish an English crowd—the means adopted by the well-matched couples being very effective, if somewhat primitive. Such simple devices as seizing one's opponent's reins, or lashing him in the face to keep him back, or pushing or pulling him off his saddle, are considered fair and legal means in order to win the race. The last heat is usually the most exciting, especially for the spectators, for blows with the lash are exchanged in bewildering profusion by both riders taking part in it, their respective ponies sharing unsparingly in the punishment. Occasionally the race becomes a regular hippic wrestling match, when both riders, clinging tightly together, tumble over and roll to the ground. When the ponies are recaptured, the bruised horsemen remount and continue the race as if nothing had happened.

The heavy sheepskin coats worn by the Tibetans are some protection when the lash is applied, and the pain inflicted is not always in proportion to the noise made by the blow; but such is not the case when they catch one another across the face.

The winner is presented with a *kata* by the umpire—a high Lama or a military officer, a most picturesque creature in a brilliant red coat and fluffy hat, who has a peculiar standard with hundreds of long, vari-coloured strips of cloth, or flying prayers. Sitting on a handsome pony, with gaudy harness of green leather inlaid with brass, a valuable Chinese rug upon the saddle, and many tinkling bells round the pony's neck, the umpire and his pony certainly produce a gay *ensemble.* This gentleman takes himself very seriously, and seldom condescends to smile.

The *kata*, or "scarf of love and friendship," which is given to the winner is a long piece of silk-like gauze, the ends of which have been trimmed into a fringe. As I have elsewhere described at greater length, these *katas* play quite an important part in the social intercourse of Tibetans. They can be purchased or obtained from the Lamas of any monastery, or where no monastery exists the natives manufacture them themselves, for they are constantly needed. No gift can be sent nor accepted without "a veil of friendship" accompanying it, and no stranger ever enters a tent without offering, with outstretched hands, a *kata*, which he quickly lays at the feet of his host. Diminutive *katas* are enclosed in letters; sweethearts exchange *katas* on every possible occasion—until they are actually married. Polyandry being prevalent in Tibet, when one of the several husbands returns to his wife after the customary absence, he never fails to bring a *kata* with him. Not to offer a *kata* to an honoured visitor is as palpable a breach of manners, and as great a slight as can possibly be offered in the Forbidden Land.

Necessarily, when a *kata* has been blessed by the Lamas, or is won in a race before high officials, it has additional value, and these simple folks value it more than a gift of money or food. It is stored away in the tent among the heirlooms, and is handed down to posterity.

A slightly more difficult feat, very common in a similar form in most countries, is the picking up of a *kata* by horsemen at full gallop. One horseman, a high official, revolves the *kata* seven times in the wind, and then darts full gallop in one direction, followed by twenty, thirty, or more horsemen riding wildly, and each trying to push his neighbours out of the way. The official, some thirty yards ahead, flies the *kata* in the wind, and when fancy takes him lets it drop out of his hand. The *kata* eventually settles on the ground, and the horde of riders gallops away from it, yelling and quarrelling. At a signal from the officer the horsemen turn round and make a dash for the scarf, towards which all the ponies are converging. Clinging to the saddle with one hand and hanging over, each rider attempts to pick up the *kata* without dismounting. Collisions and nasty falls are numerous, and this sport generally partakes of the character of an all-round fight among the ponies' legs. Somebody, however, always succeeds in picking up the scarf and getting clear of the others, when he triumphantly rides round the camp fluttering the prize in the wind.

Some of the younger fellows are clever at this sport, and when one rider at a time does the feat, he seldom misses picking up the *kata* at the first swoop.

An interesting and more difficult feat of horsemanship I witnessed in Tibet was the loading and firing of a matchlock while at full gallop—a performance which requires a firmer seat on the saddle than appears. The heavy and cumbersome weapons had to be unslung from the shoulders, the props let down, the fuse lighted by flint and steel, some gunpowder placed and kept in the small side receptacle, and last, but not least, the shot fired off—that

A RACE FOR THE *KATA*

A. H. SAVAGE LANDOR

is to say, when it would go off! The full use of both hands was required in this exercise, and therefore the horsemen held the reins with their teeth. When firing they lay almost flat on the ponies' backs in order to prevent being thrown by the sudden bucking of the frightened ponies.

Another exercise consists in bodily lifting a person on the saddle while the pony is at full gallop. The pedestrian is seized as low near the waist as possible, and the impetus of the pony's flight, not the rider's actual strength, is utilised in raising the person on the saddle.

The women seemed particularly interested in this sport, because a practical application of this exercise is used by enterprising lads of Tibet to overcome the scruples of reluctant maids who do not reciprocate their love. At a suitable opportunity the doomed young lady is abducted bodily in that fashion, and conveyed in all haste to the suitor's tent, with the honourable intention, of course, of making her his happy bride.

Women are scarce in Tibet, and actual raiding parties, I was told, occasionally take place against neighbouring tribes in order to obtain a fresh supply of wives.

Taking things all round, there are few men and

women in Tibet who cannot ride well, yet there are few who can claim exceptional skill in that line. The Tibetan generally values his bones too much to indulge in fancy tricks upon his pony. Some young fellow, more ambitious than others, will master the art of standing erect upon the saddle while going full speed, his feet being inserted into the stirrups, which have for the purpose been shortened as high as they could go. By pressing with his ankles against the saddle he manages to maintain his balance, in the familiar way of the Cossacks and tribes of Central Asia, who all excel in this game.

Tibetan saddles, as you know, are in appearance not unlike a cross between a Cossack saddle and a rude Mexican saddle, and as good as neither, but quite suited to the country where they are used. Men and women ride astride, with exceptionally short stirrups, so that the leg is bent at the knee at a right or even an acute angle. In order to maintain one's equilibrium when riding fast some additional stability is obtained by stretching out the arms sideways.

Taking all things into consideration, there is no doubt that in a rugged, mountainous country like Tibet, and for a Tibetan, his is the most practical

TIBETAN SOLDIER AT TARGET PRACTICE

and useful type of saddle, and his fashion of riding the most sensible—evidently the outcome of practical experience. When riding in caravans, driving herds of laden yaks or ponies, the advantages of legs doubled up high upon the saddle are soon apparent, avoiding the danger of crushing one's lower limbs or having them partly torn off. In the English way of riding, when among obstacles, one's legs are always in the way; in the Tibetan fashion they are always out of the way, or, at any rate, can easily and quickly be moved over from one side to the other of the saddle. Also, when tired of riding in one position, altering one's position to side-saddle is quite convenient and easy.

The blocks of the saddles are of wood imported mainly from India, Nepal, or China, with bindings of hammered iron or brass, often inlaid with silver and gold. Lizard skin and coloured leather adorn the front and back of the saddles, and a substantial pad covers the central part and the otherwise very angular seat. For extra comfort rugs—occasionally valuable and always decorative in blue and red tints—are spread, while to leather laces behind the saddle are slung double bags containing *tsamba*, *chura*, or cheese, a brick of compressed tea, and whatever sundry articles may be used on a journey.

The last, but not least attachment on a Tibetan saddle is a long coiled rope of yak hair with a wooden peg at the end for tethering the pony at night.

Whatever one may say of Tibetans, the best-inclined could not compliment them on their shooting. Their matchlocks—their only firearms, made in Lhassa and Shigatz—are weapons so clumsy and heavy and badly made, that when fired it is truly more dangerous to be behind them than in front of their muzzle. During my captivity in Tibet in 1897, indeed, I was fired upon twice—by distinguished marksmen who took accurate aim only a few paces from me—but neither time was I hit. Nor in all my experience of Tibet have I any remembrance of ever seeing a Tibetan hit with a projectile from his matchlock anything which he intended, although the range was never more than twenty or thirty yards. Few are the matchlocks in the Forbidden Land which will carry as far as fifty or a hundred yards.

They possess a long barrel, not always perfectly straight nor cylindrical; they are smooth-bore, the explosion being caused by a primitive fuse attachment which, when lighted by means of a flint and steel, applies the fire to a small cup of gunpowder at the side of the barrel. They have a peep-hole

TIBETAN WOMAN USING A SLING
FOR THROWING STONES

A.Hy SAVAGE LANDOR

sight, but this is absolutely devoid of mathematical accuracy, and the bullets and gunpowder used by the Tibetans are home-made and of inferior quality. Pebbles, or small pieces of iron, are frequently used for ammunition. A movable prop is necessary in order to enable the long weapon to be held in a horizontal position, and this should in a way facilitate accurate shooting. Apart from the various faults of the matchlocks themselves, an additional difficulty arises in Tibet even when firing with more perfected weapons. Shooting at great altitudes, it may be pointed out, involves special sighting of one's rifle; the variation in the trajectory of a projectile being considerable, at 15,000 or 16,000 feet above sea-level, owing chiefly to the rarefied air. The clearness of the atmosphere also prevents the correct estimate of range. For instance, with my ·256 Mannlicher rifle, with the usual sight at 100 yards, it was necessary at that altitude to aim about a foot lower than the target in order to make a bull's eye.

When people get to high elevations for the first time, and until they have the cause explained to them, or learn it for themselves, this is a constant puzzle, and frequently leads to the condemnation of a good weapon.

It must be said for the Tibetan that his eye is generally fairly accurate and his hand steady, and with bows and arrows I have seen some archers make quite creditable performances. These are, however, now looked upon as obsolete weapons by the natives. The soldiers as well as civilians are armed with matchlocks.

Men and women in Tibet are extremely skilful in the use of a rope sling, which they always carry about their person, and with which they can fling stones long distances with great precision. It is not uncommon, as I have said, to see them strike in this manner a picked recalcitrant sheep in a large flock, or a distant yak which they want to drive to camp. Even children, through constant practice, are adepts at stone-throwing.

All over Asia, as we have seen, is found the ancient custom of "stone-fighting," either as a sport or to settle disputes between factions; and although in Tibet these combats do not assume such gigantic proportions as in Corea, for instance, where thousands of combatants are engaged in fierce fights, still in the Forbidden Land, too, there is plenty of scope for broken skulls and bruises. The battles are generally fought between the male members of two or more rival families,

TIBETAN GAMES. STONE-THROWING

A.H. SAVAGE LANDOR

and seldom between large factions or guilds, except in big towns such as Lhassa or Shigatz, where these stone fights occasionally assume alarming proportions. They are undoubtedly a speedy and practical method of settling controversies among rival families, besides affording some considerable amusement and excitement to the gathered crowd of spectators watching the progress of the combat well out of range of the missiles.

Stone-throwing in a different form, as a sport, is indulged in on festive occasions by young men. Some large rocks, more or less spherical, and some 30 to 50 lbs. in weight, being collected, and the participants in the game having divested themselves of their heavy coats, which are left hanging from their waistbands, the rocks are lifted and swung over the head and flung some considerable distance, often ten or twelve yards, either into an appropriate hole or near a mark-stone. This exercise generally takes place near a *mani* wall, such as is represented in the illustration in this book. Another form of the same game consists in kicking to or near a particular spot a small stone with the instep of one's foot, swinging one's stiffened leg as if it were a golf-club.

Wrestling is one of the few other sports noticeable in Tibet. It is, however, not commonly indulged in, and is done according to no rules. It is, in fact, in the "catch as catch can" style, with additional biting and vicious kicking until the victor can firmly hold the helpless vanquished flat under him.

The amusement which always causes much mirth among Tibetans is tobogganing. They do not always indulge in it as a sport; but when opportunity offers, for instance, to save themselves the trouble of long and steep descents on snowy mountain slopes, they greatly enjoy the fun. I have seen Tibetans slide on their backs at a terrific pace for a hundred or two hundred yards down precipitous inclines, laughing and yelling, with their heavy sheepskin coats collected in front, and their legs up in the air except when required for steering purposes.

With the exception of the above, I do not recollect seeing any other national sport; nor, as a matter of fact, do Tibetans indulge much in sports of any kind—partly owing to the great altitudes which they inhabit, where violent exercise leads to considerable personal discomfort and suffering; partly because of a somewhat depressed nature. Although not always devoid of considerable humour,

TOBOGGANING MADE EASY

the Tibetan can seldom be roused from his normal sulkiness and made to put forth superfluous exertion either for his own delectation or that of others.

Also, the nomadic existence which he leads from one end of the year to the other, is full of ever present wild excitements and surprises. He often travels over snowy passes several thousand feet higher than the highest mountains of Europe, where precipices and avalanches and land-slides or falling rocks are of daily occurrence, and any devised sport becomes in comparison rather tame and uninteresting.

Naturally, there is no such thing in Tibet as training to be an athlete, nor are the few sports and games specially taught to the children. They are merely picked up from one generation to the other by imitation. The Tibetan is extremely hardy and wiry.

Amusements which are the result of prosperity and happiness are not plentiful in Tibet. Playing cards and dice and a primitive sort of chess, and one or two more elaborate games imported from China and Nepal, are occasionally to be seen; but perhaps the most interesting to us is their dancing, notably their war-dances, curious in people so little martial. With a sword in one hand and a *kata* in the other, and with the knees bent, the dancers keep time to the beating of a double drum and the clapping of hands from the spectators. They attempt some more or less clumsy revolutions on their heels, but the movements of their arms are quite graceful. Alternately each bent arm is raised in front of the head, while the other is held far back, and they manage to give a pretty semi-rotary twist to both forearms and hands when they have reached the highest and lowest points respectively.

As the dancers and musicians get excited the movements of the arms and legs are greatly accelerated, and some of the best dancers can move their limbs so quickly that on looking at them one's eyes get confused to such an extent that only a shapeless moving mass is distinguishable. Owing to the rarefied air, they cannot, however, keep this up very long, and, panting, their lungs in convulsion and eyes bulging out of their sockets, they abruptly end the dance with a suggestive and humorous—often too humorous—posture, or else with a leap in the air, doubling up the body and resting the head upon the knees before the feet touch the ground again.

The most appreciated dancing, from a Tibetan

TIBETAN DANCE WITH SWORD AND *KATA* (VEIL OF FRIENDSHIP)

A. HENRY SAVAGE LANDOR

point of view, is when the performer can continue his evolutions, bringing his legs forward alternately with knees bent low and almost touching the ground. In a way, this dance is not unlike Russian peasant dancing. The best dancers give solo performances, while the rest join in a circle round and round them until they get tired out and dizzy.

The women's dancing has precisely the same characteristics, except that it is done with no sword. Only a *kata* is held in the right hand, and the contortions are less exaggerated, and, therefore, more graceful. The abrupt end also is done away with, together with odd posturing. The women, whenever I saw them dance, usually danced singly to the accompaniment of softer and more sentimental music than was the case with the men. They added sad, melodious chanting to their movements, weird and wild to a degree, yet full of expression and quite pleasing to the ear.

CHAPTER XV

THE Tibetan in his normal life is occasionally an amusing being, full of coarse humour, and with a bounce which carries him through his existence. When alone, he is quiet in his manner, and will spend his leisure hours spinning wool or in some other such feminine occupation, while his women-folk do all the hard work about the tent. As will be seen by the illustrations in this book, both Tibetan men and women look clumsy and heavy. Anatomically, they are well-built, small but wiry, and rather thickly set, but very seldom with any great abundance of flesh and fat, except the Lamas, who lead a lascivious and lazy life.

Tibetan clothing is mostly responsible for the funny appearance they present, men wearing sometimes three or four coats, skin or woollen, one on the top of the other. The sash or belt, which is intended to be at the waist, is usually considerably

A TYPICAL TIBETAN

A.H. SAVAGE LANDOR

lower down owing to the weight of the variety of articles the wearer constantly carries stored away round the waist in his outer coat,—wooden bowls, balls of butter, bags of *tsamba*, a bundle of wool for spinning with the distaff, the prayer-wheel, and a quantity of rags,—which bulge out at the waist all round his body and drag down his coat. This often gives them the appearance of being quite short-legged, though, of course, they are not really.

Men and women wear picturesque, most comfortable and practical long boots, the legging being usually red or white, the thick soles of rope well protecting the foot all round. These boots are largely manufactured in Lhassa and Shigatz, but people also manufacture them themselves. Officials wear leather boots of the Chinese type, with thick wooden or leather soles with a few huge iron nails underneath and a curled-up toe.

Among the coloured illustrations will be found paintings of Tibetan women—from babyhood, in an ample and striking robe of white and blue checks; at the age of twelve, with shaggy hair hanging down the back and shoulders and a sufficient collection of ornaments round the neck; an older dame, of middle class and age, in her everyday costume, with a sash enveloping nearly one-third of her body; then a lady of rank and beauty, fully decorated with amber necklace, gold and malachite brooch, elaborate earrings, and a much-adorned aureole upon the head. She sits modestly on bags of borax, and displays feet of some considerable size. Well, that is the fault of the ample and padded boots which she wears, and not a fault of the foot inside—not small, mind you, but generally well-formed—nor of the painter who depicted the scene.

Next we have a religious lady praying before a tent shrine, turning her back to us and displaying in its full glory her *Tchukti*—that is to say, three broad bands of three sections each alternately blue and red. These bands of heavy cloth reach from the shoulder to the feet, and they are ornamented with coral or malachite beads, silver coins and bells, and at the lower end a row of little brass or silver bells is generally attached. Nearly all the money earned by the woman (and frequently that of the husband) is sewn on to the *Tchukti*, so that the family fortune — when this fortune exists—hangs down women's backs to a number of neat little tresses of the woman's hair to which it is attached. When the *Tchukti* is worn the hair is parted in the middle and plastered down with melted butter.

Last, but not least, you will find the portrait of a Tibetan old lady, who somewhat resented being sketched and had not her sweetest smile upon her face. Rather bony and toothless, with a wrinkled skin which would put to shame a crocodile, one leg stretched out because she had a rheumatic pain and could not bend it, she used quite bad language when I quickly portrayed her. She predicted and wished misfortunes of all kinds which should descend upon me.

Perhaps you will notice, in most of the illustrations representing Tibetans, that the people depicted in them have their eyes half-closed. This is one of the most characteristic points about a Tibetan face, especially when out of doors and conversing. First of all, as you know, the Mongolian eye is elongated between heavy lids, and does not afford an extensive view of the iris at any time; then, owing to the intensely brilliant light, the severe and constant winds, and plentiful snow, the natives get into the habit of accentuating the squeezing of the eye-aperture for protection. This causes crow's-feet to appear on men and women at an early age, and a much corrugated forehead and brow.

I had occasion on this journey to pay a visit to

a quaint tribe of Tibetans calling themselves the Kam-par, or people from Kam (Tibet). They possessed extraordinary features — from intermarriage with some tribe of Nepal, I should think —intensely cruel faces in many instances; others quite refined, especially those of the better class. The young man whose portrait I give, very girlish-looking, with an elaborate hat ornamented with gold embroidery, was the son of the chief, and quite a nice-looking boy, with suave manners and a humble voice. He had long hair in waves upon his shoulders, and a short pigtail behind. But some of the older men, such as the one I portrayed, had brutal faces, and their manner was somewhat coarse, sulky, and blunt. They possessed highly developed cheek-bones, slits of eyes, and prominent drooping lips. The nose, however, was more developed than on other Tibetans.

These people, like most other Tibetans, practise a form of cannibalism which is not at all uncommon in Tibet, especially in their funeral ceremonies. The Lamas, as is well known, often drink human blood out of bowls made of human skulls.

This tribe, a nomad one, was, among other employments, given to a certain amount of brigandage;

WOMAN AND CHILD PRAYING BEFORE
A SHRINE INSIDE A TENT

LANDOR

and, in fact, among them I found a well-known brigand—a long-lost friend of mine—whose portrait I also give in these pages. He possessed quite a striking-looking head, with a good deal of determination upon his features, a fierce moustache, and masses of curly hair trimmed straight at the height of the shoulders. He always shouted at the top of his voice whenever he spoke; always heartily laughed at everything you said; and, to show his approval, struck you upon your shoulder with his ponderous hand after each sentence. He was one of the most powerfully built men I have ever met, his strength being quite extraordinary; and, for a brigand, quite an agreeable companion out of business hours.

Polyandry, when the wife is shared among brothers, as is the case all over Tibet, is practised by this tribe also; and when I met them they were employed in conveying salt and borax from Gyanema over the Darma Pass into India. These Kam-par occasionally travel as far down as Tanakpore, the borax and salt being carried entirely on sheep-back.

When one got over the peculiar expression of their faces, the Kam-par were amiable enough.

Their women were highly decorated with

numerous brass ornaments with pendants, and silver bracelets inlaid with malachite. Teeth of musk-deer were freely used as ornaments, as well as being used for such useful purposes as picking one's teeth, cleaning the nails, and so on.

The chief wore his hair parted in the centre, and plaited into small tresses which joined into a single pigtail behind. The skin was of a sallow yellowish colour. The upper portion of the eye, as is often the case in people who are constantly exposed to a brilliant light, was much discoloured, and a peculiar whitish tinge veiled the entire iris of the eye. In the way of clothing they showed a marked preference for bright red and yellow textiles, and on their visits into Kumaon they had invested their savings in buying old regimental brass buttons, with which the women were freely ornamented. Bracelets of glass beads, and also necklaces of coral and amber, were displayed with pride.

These people had beautiful tents, the inside being most comfortable, with Chinese carpets spread on the floor, cushions to rest the head and back upon, and cured skins spread everywhere where they might come in useful. Elaborate altars, some double-tiered, with as many as seven images of Buddha, were to be seen, and upon them

TIBETAN BOY IN HIS GOLD-EMBROIDERED HAT

A. Henry Savage Landor

burning lights galore, incense-sticks alight filling the tent with saintly fumes. Bags of butter and *chura* and sweet paste hung from every tent-pole. All round the tent, inside and also outside, were high walls of double sacks of borax. Outside, on high posts, with an ingenious contrivance to prevent animals going up, a lot of meat was prepared, with salt, in thin slices, and exposed to the sun to dry.

As is always the case, with this tribe too travelled a number of Lamas, who practically controlled everything. One of these Lamas had as repulsive and murderous a face as it is given to any human being to possess. True enough, his first boast was that he had killed three people (the natives said a good many more). His manner towards the people was most brutal. He was a tall man of marvellous muscular development, and between his most repulsive lips, which never seemed to close, he displayed a set of most powerful long pointed teeth, such as those one would see in a wild animal. His head-gear consisted of a vizor made of long, bristly hair—not unlike the half of a chimney-sweeper's brush—which he fastened round the forehead and back of the head with a string.

This gentleman was inclined to be overbearing,

even intrusive; and, to show his courage as well as muscular power (possibly to frighten me), he thumped and knocked about his people in a merciless manner, always taking care to select the helpless and weaker ones. His brutality irritated me considerably. I was standing near his tent, and he came in with a long knife—he had been making himself a stick to beat the people with. He was still foaming with rage. There was a woman, his servant, sitting near the fire, and he asked her whether the tea was ready in the *raksang*. She replied it was not, upon which he administered a terrific kick in her stomach which would have killed any woman but a Tibetan. I could stand no more. I seized my rifle by the muzzle and applied the butt upon his face in a fashion which somewhat flattened his nose more than it originally was and loosened some teeth. All bullies are cowards in any country, and he made no reply whatever.

No doubt I shall be blamed—as I have been before—for administering my own justice in other people's countries, but I cannot help feeling that the weak should ever and at any cost be protected against unwarranted attacks of the brutally strong.

Another similar, but more comical, incident—

A BRIGAND

A. Hy. SAVAGE LANDOR

one of many—occurred another day, when a shapeless figure, almost bent over in two and walking unsteadily upon his feet, approached my camp. We were in a barren, desolate spot, cold and dreary, and my men had put up *chokdens* of stones all round the camp.

The queer stranger had a most comical appearance, his waist down to his knees, so full was his coat with stores of all kinds. He bowed profusely, his shaggy hair flying—as much as it could fly, for it was so dirty and entangled—in the breeze.

"Who are you and what do you want?" we asked him.

"I am a poor, poor man, with no food and no friends."

I well knew this to be a lie, as I had had similar visitors before. He was a mere Tibetan spy—a soldier in the disguise of a beggar, to come and find out all about us.

"What do you want?"

"I am hungry and have pains in my inside for lack of food."

I ordered my cook to give him plentiful meat and rice and some sweet paste. A little of it he ate; the rest he stored away in his coat, wrapped up in dirty rags.

"Is there anything else you want?"

"Yes, I would like some *tchah* (tea)."

A jug of tea was handed him.

"Anything else you wish from us now?" we inquired of the Tibetan, who, while pretending to sip the tea, was counting the number of my men, was trying to see how many rifles we had, and was taking in everything all round with his ferreting eyes. But although he was a splendid actor, his infirmities, I had detected at once, were all put on for the occasion.

"Can I be allowed to prowl around your camp and see what I can pick up—anything you have thrown away?"

"Yes, certainly; but mind you do not pick more than you expect."

The man crawled about camp—I ordered my men to pretend not to notice him—while I observed him closely, all the time pretending to be busy writing. By means of a small looking-glass I could watch his movements even when he was behind me. The fellow was examining all my baggage carefully, and especially our rifles which lay about. Having persuaded himself that none of us were looking at him, he raised the flap of my tent and had a good look inside. When he

A TIBETAN SPY IN THE DISGUISE OF
A BEGGAR APPROACHING THE
AUTHOR'S CAMP

A. Hy Savage Landor

had finished his inspection he came to bid me good-bye.

"Have you had all you want, do you think?" I asked him.

"Yes, indeed. He was grateful. He now wanted to go."

"Before you go, *I* want to give you a remembrance to teach you that when you accept people's hospitality you should not practise treachery."

Snatching out of his hand a long stick he carried, I applied to him a good beating—not that it hurt him much, because he was so padded with articles he had stored in his coat. In fact, in trying to struggle away, his sash got undone and he dropped a number of little bags containing *tsamba* and butter, provisions which were evidently intended to last him several days on his spying expedition. Also two daggers.

My men, who entered fully into the spirit of the joke, chased him out of camp with a well-directed shower of stones. Needless to say, "the starving Tibetan cripple" outran them all. From a high point of vantage I watched him with my telescope. When some distance off he went among some rocks, picked up his matchlock which he had hidden there—and continued his flight.

CHAPTER XVI

As you know, the Tibetans when saluting put out the tongue to its full extent. If they are wearing a cap it is removed and placed upon the ground in sign of respect, especially if the person saluted is of high social standing. The hands, joined with the thumbs together and raised, are waved up and down in front of the forehead.

There is a code of social etiquette among Tibetans even of the most degraded tribes. For instance, it is not customary to enter a tent without first announcing one's presence and demanding admittance. Also, no Tibetan traveller, except Government messengers, will enter an encampment after dark unless he has warned the inhabitants beforehand.

It must not be argued that because the officials of Tibet—the Lamas particularly—show intense cruelty, especially to foreigners, everybody in

"CHAKZAL, CHAKZAL"

The Tibetan salutation consists in putting out the tongue to its full length.

Tibet is cruel. On the contrary, there are many folks in Tibet who possess generous hearts. The people are charitable to a degree, even the poorest sharing what little they have with strangers poorer than themselves. During my captivity in Tibet, on my first expedition, on many occasions individual Tibetans showed sympathy and consideration, when, had it been discovered, it would have cost them their heads. So that, after all, not all Tibetans are bad. If anything—barring the Lamas—the people are rather good-natured and easygoing, easily led and influenced if taken the right way.

Tibetan men are not fighting men, and are, perhaps, the most contemptible cowards in face of danger. Curiously enough, it is not fear of death which makes them pusillanimous, but apparently the notion of getting hurt and the absolute lack of resolution. If ordered by his superiors and impressed with the idea that if killed by the enemy he will find himself in heaven, whereas if he bolts and returns to camp he will be beheaded and go to a hell of ice and snow—yes, the Tibetan hell is a cool place; but their heaven is warm, with splendid grazing for yaks!—then, indeed, a Tibetan will stand helplessly to be shot without defending himself, while Maxim guns and shrapnel and other things of the kind are playing upon him. The carnages of the British Tibet Mission, of which we importers of civilisation should not feel too proud, are a good instance of this.

So, again, although a contemptible coward, he does not fear death. I myself, while in Tibet, could confirm this statement by many personal experiences. When officials came to induce me to leave the country they maintained, and it was true, that they had strict orders from Lhassa to drive me away. If they returned unsuccessful from their mission they would, they declared, be beheaded. When I insisted on continuing my journey they frequently handed me their sword, requesting me to cut off their head then and there, which would save them the dishonour of degradation and a public execution.

Once or twice, as the Tibetans on my first journey had given me a taste of what it felt like to be taken out to the execution ground and have a sword flourished round my neck, I thought that I was fully entitled to try a practical joke and see what effect the similar sensation would have on Tibetan officers. Only, of course, in my case I had not asked to be beheaded, and therefore the process came more as a surprise, besides being

A PICTURESQUE OLD FELLOW

carried out in dead earnest up to, but fortunately with a postponement of, the last stroke.

To go on with my narrative, I pretended to accept the offer of the Tibetan officers, and, calling all my men, lined them up to witness the execution. The Tibetan officers knelt down, somewhat trembling but quite resigned, and cleared their necks to make my work easy. Many of them did not flinch, but some did when I approached, brandishing the sword in their own fashion; and, by Jove! the latter proved themselves to be the champion runners of the country. Naturally, I never injured these fellows in any way, and when they showed any determination at all I always gave them a suitable present of some sort or other.

After the performance was over they fully entered into the humour of the joke themselves, and we used to have very hearty laughs over it, and endless cups of tea.

When you travel in Tibet you see, in the daytime, men and women garbed in heavy skin coats; only one sleeve at a time is put on while half the chest and the other arm are left bare. This, to any one not suspecting the reason, looks very incongruous, and has led to all sorts of ridiculous explanations from the usual theoretical scientists at home. The real explanation is simple and is this.

As I have elsewhere explained, the heat of the sun is in Tibet very great—especially in Southern Tibet,—the latitude not being many degrees north, and the power of the sun's rays is even intensified by the clearness of the rarefied air. On the other hand, owing to the immense elevation, the cold is intense wherever the sun does not strike, so that it is not uncommon to feel absolutely roasted on the sunny side and frozen on the other. Hence the necessity of having winter clothing to cover half your anatomy, while the other half demands nothing more than tropical bareness.

The Tibetans are not artistic by nature. Their art is of the most rudimentary kind. A few earthen pots, graceful enough in shape, but of no extraordinary beauty, are manufactured by them, and some brass and iron vessels are made in the cities. Also, of course, in a population of several millions there have been a few individuals who have attempted more ambitious works of art, such as paintings (mostly of religious subjects) and sculptures, but although in the paintings the colouring is bright, and much care is devoted to

AN AMBIDEXTER LAMA SCULPTOR
CARVING AN INSCRIPTION ON
THE FACE OF A ROCK

A.H. SAVAGE LANDOR

details, anatomical accuracy and proportion are always lacking in the figures, and not even a shade of perspective is to be noticed in their landscapes. In certain conventional decorative ways, however, the Tibetans are quite masters, as, for instance, in the gigantic religious inscriptions one frequently finds all over the country upon dangerous vertical cliffs. One of the coloured plates given in this book represents a young Lama—the Lamas can always be distinguished in Tibet by their clean-shaven heads—inscribing the words "*Omni mani padmi hun*" upon the face of a rock. The work is carried on at a great height, the artist being suspended in a rope sling. Lamas with any special talent in this direction are kept in monasteries and sent all over the country to adorn the barren landscape, especially on high caravan routes, with these sacred characters. Perhaps, when Tibet has been fully opened to foreign civilisation, these talents will find a more remunerative occupation in substituting for the sacred words advertisements of fancy soaps and hair restorers.

These sculptors, and, in fact, most of the cleverer Tibetans, are practically ambidexter, being able to use either hand, especially in works which require no great delicacy of touch. As can be seen in the illustration, the young Lama is using the hammer with his left hand.

The cloth made by Tibetans is of great strength, especially fabrics of yak hair, but seldom of a handsome design. Very irregular designs are occasionally attempted, but usually the Tibetan woman is wise enough never to depart from the striped pattern. Tibetan fabrics are generally woven too narrow for any practical use in European countries.

CHAPTER XVII

PERHAPS some of the experiences we had on our trip across country may interest the reader. Instead of returning by Tinker we proceeded in a north-westerly direction, employing an old man—a most peculiar fellow, so wrinkled that he seemed almost mummified—who said he knew the way across the intricate ranges. When we had nearly reached the summit of the range, we came in for a very bad storm, a regular blizzard, and it delayed us for some hours. My guide, as is usual with guides, lost his head, and, what was worse, also his way. We could not remain where we were, and we could not see where we were going.

I took matters into my own hands, and, by compass, tried to find my way to where I supposed the place was; but we experienced great difficulty in getting along, owing to the snow being driven with great force into our faces and obscuring the view a few yards away from us. I found the pass right enough, the blizzard abating for a few moments, and we sank in soft snow up to our knees, which made marching very heavy. We descended a few hundred feet and found ourselves in a sort of gully, which necessitated making another ascent to a higher and more difficult pass before we could descend into the valley where the sources of the Ganges are to be found.

Night was coming on fast, my men were in a pitiable condition from fatigue and cold, and the wind blew the ground-snow—frozen into grains like sand—in regular whirlwinds round us, which pretty well blinded us. I was ahead of my party with two men, struggling up the steep incline, when some of those in the rear shouted that three of my men had remained behind and were missing. They were no longer answering the signals we constantly made in order not to lose one another. This necessitated a long delay and a search being made for them. One of the pictures in this book shows us shouting to them in order to find their whereabouts, but we shouted ourselves hoarse and got no answer. I detailed two of my best men to go back to find them, and provided them with extra blankets, as they would very likely spend

A WEIRD OLD MAN OF N.W. NEPAL

A. Hy SAVAGE LANDOR

the night up there and not catch us up till the next day. I also left the mummified guide with them.

We went on and eventually got over the higher and more difficult pass before it got too dark, the wind blowing so hard that we had at times great difficulty in proceeding against it. The descent was most dangerous, the snow was treacherous, and when we got lower down we got among a lot of loose boulders and dangerous sheets of ice, which gave us no end of trouble. We were benighted, and it got so dark that we did not see where we were putting our feet, which, half-frozen as they were, constantly got jammed and knocked and bruised. Some of the rounder boulders frequently rolled under us as we trod on them, and caused us very nasty falls. At each step we unavoidably started a regular landslip of rocks and *débris*, rolling down the steep mountain side, the *fracas* of which, with the howling of the wind, made quite a diabolical noise.

The lower we got, the warmer it became, and, of course, the snow lessened and eventually disappeared. We travelled for a long distance along the bed of a river, and, farther on, upon what seemed the ancient bed of a lake, an immense, flat stretch of gravel.

Having got among some big boulders, which necessitated a lot of fatiguing work on all fours, one of my men, in trying to help me to get down a big rock, slipped, and dragged me with him, a jump of some 15 feet. As I fell on my back, I was considerably shaken, while my man injured his arm rather badly.

A little later, having reached the camping ground of Dongan, we halted and pitched our tents at four o'clock in the morning. It was not till late in the day that the missing men and those sent to their relief arrived in a pitiable condition. They had been compelled to abandon two loads. One man was badly frost-bitten, another taken with such violent cramps and pains in his inside that I had grave fears for his recovery. He had to be carried, which involved a terrible tax on my other men, who were all much worn and footsore.

Our march the previous day had been over twenty-two miles. Dongan was only 14,100 feet above sea-level, and we felt comparatively comfortable and warm. We had three high peaks to 80°, 100°, 125° b.m., and to the north-west was the Lippu Lekh, 16,780 feet.

I revisited the source of the Ganges, a pretty

OVER A PASS IN A COMING STORM

little spot where a limpid spring gurgles out from under a big boulder, and forms a crystal-like pool adorned with *chokdens.* This water is deliciously cool, and very nearly caused the death of three of my Hindoo men. They drank copiously while soaked in perspiration, and washed themselves prior to eating their food. They were seized with a colic accompanied by high fever, and they groaned in their contortions upon the ground. We applied massage freely and violent rubbing, which, with an additional quick cure of my own, is very successful on such occasions; and eventually—after some hours—they were able to continue, although still suffering.

Partly owing to the strain being over, partly owing to the intense sufferings of the previous day, and the excessive eating to celebrate the temporary end of our troubles, three more men were taken very ill on our way up the Kuti valley, and I had to send them down into Garbyang.

I was now again in Bias, a portion of the country practically ceded that year by the British Government to Tibet. In fact, Tibetan emissaries had been in all the villages—Gungi, Nabi, Ronkan, and Kuti—imposing upon the natives in every way, claiming taxes and proclaiming Tibetan sovereignty.

At Kuti, where I arrived, as usual, in the middle of the night, owing to the long marches we did daily, I had the surprise and pleasure of meeting Nattalì again, one of the strongest-willed, noblest-minded, pluckiest, and sweetest little ladies I have ever met. She was a Kutial Shoka, and as pretty as they make them. Her grace of manner, her inconceivable thoughtfulness and absolute purity of thought were enough to put to shame many a woman of more civilised countries.

Being a lady of wealth, for a Shoka—for her husband was one of the big traders of the district—she owned the finest house in Kuti. She would not hear of our remaining under canvas, and insisted on evacuating the house to let us occupy it. Not only that, but the poor thing sat up half the night to prepare sweets and all sorts of luxuries for our benefit, and I had a great struggle the next day—even the sweetest woman can be obstinate—to make her accept a sufficient remuneration for her trouble.

Both Tibetan emissaries and men from the British Political Agent were hiding in the village in order to attempt wrecking my expedition and stirring the natives up against me; in fact, the people were most turbulent in the morning, and I

CALLING TWO FOLLOWERS LOST IN THE STORM

thought we should come in for a good fight. We had to knock about some of the villagers, who seemed morose and inclined to give trouble, and at one moment it looked as if a general battle might result. Stones were thrown at us, and we thought we had better disperse the crowd before it got too formidable. While my men pounded away on some of the more excited folks and drove them back, Nattalì stood by me and gave her rebellious countrymen such sonorous cracks on the head with a heavy stick—heavens! was she not quick with her hands!—that I had to sit down on a stone, in convulsions of laughter. Then she even persuaded a number of Kutials to enter my employ and accompany me. Others who refused to come she called cowards, spat upon them, and again gave them a taste of the stick. I liked her very much for that.

A relative of hers, whom she particularly warned to be faithful to me, proved himself one of the most hard-working and devoted followers I have ever had.

I well remember her, the day we left. She, with a great many villagers, came to accompany us to the boundary of their village, a high point from which an extensive view is obtained of the upper course of the Kuti River along which we were to travel. Having bade us a melancholy good-bye—for she had a presentiment that we should have great trouble before us—she sat herself upon a rock, resting her placid little face upon her hands, and she remained watching us until we were out of sight. Every now and then we waved our hands at her, and her little arm waved a parting salute against the bright line of the sky. That was the last we saw of Nattalì.

By a most remarkable coincidence, as I sat down in my London rooms to jot down these words for publication—now five years later,—as I was writing the word "Nattalì" upon the paper a letter from India was handed to me. On opening it, it contained the sad news that Nattalì was dead.

TIBETAN GOAT

CHAPTER XVIII

THE corrected elevation of the Kuti village by boiling-point thermometers is 12,554 feet—possibly one of the highest villages in the world.

It was my intention to go up the Kuti River in a north-west direction and cross over the Lebung Pass into the Darma district, in the northern part of which I wanted to explore some glaciers and passes. The way up the Kuti River was naturally very rough, but we had no great difficulty; and as my own men were refreshed, and I also had excellent additional followers and lavish food for everybody, everything went well enough until we reached Jolinkan.

The Government *chaprassis* whom I had taken prisoners were getting very anxious, now that they saw before them another prospect of camping on snow and ice, and endeavoured to escape. I stopped them in time, and warned them very seriously. With long, depressed faces they swore they would not leave me till it pleased me to deliver them in person to their superior officer.

We had brought up some sheep, carrying loads of food, and their services answered a double purpose. When the loads were consumed the transport animals provided nourishing diet for my men.

Our camp at the foot of the Lebung Pass was 14,913 feet above sea-level.

We here abandoned the Kuti River, and after a good night's rest proceeded to ascend the Lebung Pass, by which we were to cross the high range separating the valley of Darma from that of the Kuti River. Along this range, a spur from the Himahlyan main backbone running somewhat tortuously in a general south-east direction, are several peaks rising to great elevations: 20,760 feet, 20,250 feet, 20,324 feet, 20,386 feet, 20,328 feet, 20,264 feet, 20,455 feet. The ascent on the east side was very steep, but presented no great difficulty, although my men suffered considerably owing to having over-eaten themselves the previous night and in the morning before starting.

On the pass, 19,016 feet, we erected a cairn, and I took observations on most of my men.

A TROUBLESOME DESCENT ON VERTICAL ROCKS

They nearly all suffered from mountain sickness, and the pulse of all was much accelerated. The highest registered 126, 118, 134, 108 pulsations. The average pulsations of these men at the altitude where they lived was from 66 to 90. The usual symptoms were present: a very warm forehead, pains and vigorous thumping at the temples, pressure and aches in the top and back of head. Curiously enough, when the pain in the temples was only on one side, it was generally on the right side of the head. Occasionally this pain extended all along the posterior fissure of the cranium. Heart-throbbing as well as thumping in the centre of the chest were general, and great sleepiness and exhaustion prevailed among them. The pupils of the eyes were abnormally contracted, almost to the size of the point of a pin.

When we had rested sufficiently we found ourselves confronted with rather a trying task. On the other side of the pass of rotten rock, several hundred feet in height, not unlike what we had met on the Savage Pass, was a precipitous wall, requiring somewhat of a steady head and endless labour in getting over. Perhaps a glance at the illustration depicting the scene will give a better idea of the situation than a long description.

My men can be seen conveying down the baggage —a most tedious and long performance, each package being passed down from one man to another stationed at intervals along the vertical rock. As the distance was considerable and the men few, each man had to undergo considerable exertion and a lot of climbing up and down to collect from the man above and deliver each load to his neighbour below. So that to go those few hundred yards took us several hours. The sheep accompanying us, too, had to be carried down one by one, and in some places let down by means of rope slings.

We had passed a small glacier on the east watershed of the pass, and now we had below us to the south-west the great Lebung Glacier, feeding the Dholi Ganga by two or three streamlets. We skirted it to the north on a lot of *débris*. The main portion had a general direction from north-east to south-west, then an arm extended due west. In the latter portion of the glacier were big cracks in the ice, while to the north-west was an immense dune of ice, mud, and *débris*, forming a line from 30° to 231°. From this point of observation the Lebung Pass stood at 210° b.m. There were fine terraces in this glacier, supported on a high wall of ice and mud. To the south-east could be seen one of the high snowy peaks towering over the Rama Glacier to the south of the Lebung.

The Darma Valley, in which we now found ourselves, takes its name from the Darma Yangti, a river which has its birth at the foot of the Lumpiya Pass, and is further fed by the tributary streams from glaciers on either side.

The Darma Parganah was of some interest to me, as one of the minor routes into Tibet was along this river. Darma proper was divided into two divisions : the Malla and the Talla, or "upper" and "lower," Darma. The Malla Darma is that portion which comprises the Lissar River and the Dholi Ganga, whereas the Talla Darma, as its name suggests, lies nearer to the point at which the Dholi Ganga meets the Kali River.

The Darma Shokas, a tribe somewhat differing from the Shokas of Bias and Chaudas, carry on the entire trade with Tibet by the Darma route. Gyanema is the main centre, and the commodities are chiefly borax, salt, wool, skins, cloth, and utensils, in exchange for which the Tibetans receive silver, wheat, rice, *satoo*, *ghur*, candied sugar, pepper, beads of all kinds, and a few articles of Indian manufacture.

It was getting towards the end of September when I was in this region, and the weather was very cold and stormy. We had plenty of snow every night and the winds were cutting. It was a great temptation, I must confess, when we reached the Dholi River, to turn towards the south, which would bring us to lower elevations and therefore to warmth and comfort; but my work was not finished, and we had again to go towards the north (N.N.W., to be strictly accurate), for I wished to solve certain geographical problems and visit some passes into the Forbidden Land which I had not yet ascended.

We camped that night at a dreary spot called Gankan (12,295 feet), where we expected to find some traders, this being one of their temporary stations, but did not. So we fared rather badly. We could find no fuel, and the supply which they generally bring up with them was quite exhausted. All the trading with Tibet was now over from this side, and everybody had retired southward. Two stray sheep—one dead, the other still alive but with broken legs—were lying near the wall which marked the favourite spot for a camping-ground. We passed a very chilly night, and the next day when we woke snow was falling heavily. My

A PHANTOM LION OF GIGANTIC PROPORTIONS

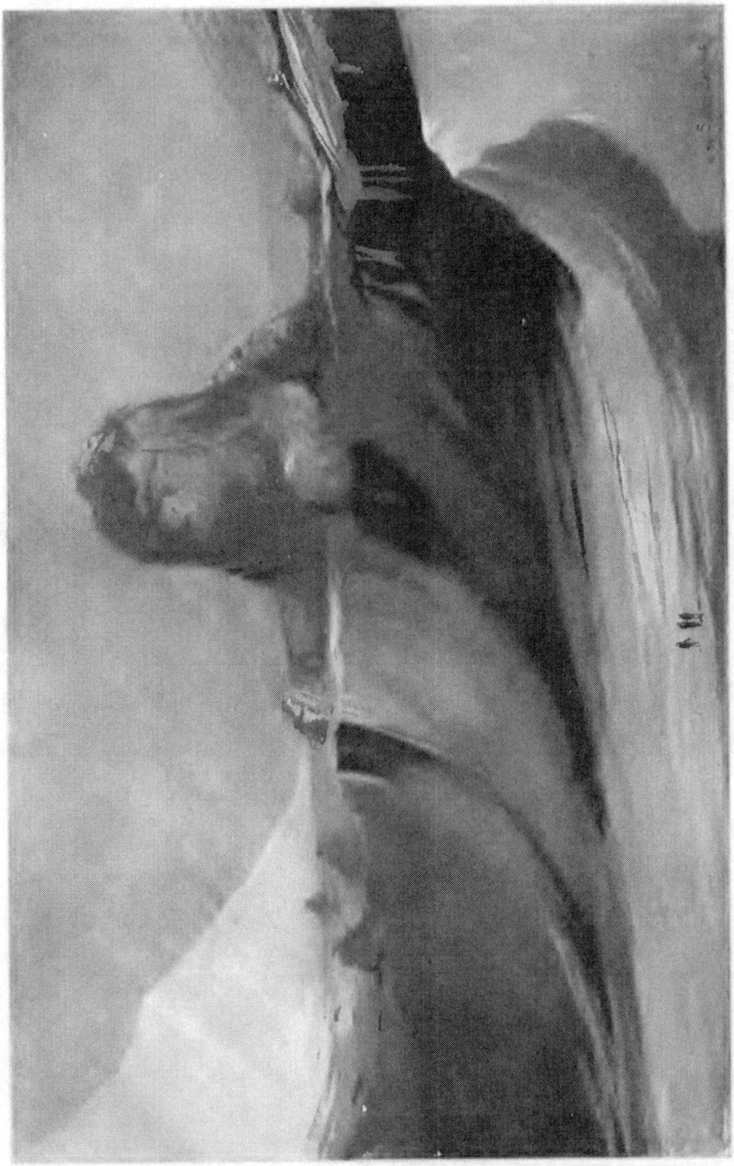

men seemed to be sufferingly greatly, and I decided to ask for two volunteers to accompany me and carry my instruments to the glaciers northwards, the remainder of the expedition proceeding one march southward, to a place where fuel could be obtained, and awaiting our return there.

We three started off in a fierce wind at six o'clock in the morning, and passed three small glaciers to the east—the Suiti, Pungrung, and Mangti. To the west were five other smaller glaciers. We had gradually risen to 15,000 feet, and farther on, at the foot of the Nui Glacier, at the spot known as the Nui Encamping-ground, the altitude was 16,950 feet.

It was at this place that, in the mist and snow, we saw the immense image of what seemed a conventional crouching lion sculptured in the rock. On approaching it, however, the illusion was explained. The main body—as I have already explained—was merely a gigantic boulder, while the extended paws and tail were *mani* walls with end *chokdens* built away from the rock. From a certain point of view it looked exactly like a lion.

This being the last camp before traders attempt the high pass, many *chokdens* of all sizes are to be seen all over the valley and on the hill-side. One of the peculiarities of these *chokdens* is that they are as much as possible built with white or light-coloured stones.

The wind had got much worse as we got higher, and the effort of walking was considerable. We had gone some eleven miles, and my two men were so exhausted they were unable to continue. They dragged along uncomplainingly, but I could see that they were on the verge of breaking down. At the foot of the Nui we had some food, and having laden myself with all the necessary instruments and cameras—quite a considerable weight—I left my two men to await my return, while I went alone to survey the Nui Glacier and climb the high pass.

Once alone, I proceeded at a greater speed, but the ground was much broken by huge boulders, and to cover a short distance involved a lot of labour. About one mile and a half from where I had left my men I came in for an experience which I did not quite expect at that moment, although, fortunately, I was prepared for any emergency.

The Tibetans had had time to prepare a great many snares for me, and to send soldiers to all the passes, and what they could not do by facing me direct they attempted as usual to accomplish by treachery. Much to my astonishment in this desolate region, I came upon a Tibetan comfortably seated upon the ground, upon which he had spread several coats. I asked him if he were alone, and he said yes.

"What are you doing here?"

"I am going back to my country. My friends went ahead yesterday."

"Surely you have some one with you; you cannot carry all those coats and paraphernalia?"

"No, no no; I am quite alone."

As I was standing talking to him I noticed that his eyes were looking at something behind me, and on turning round found myself confronted with three Tibetans, who had evidently crawled out from behind rocks where they were hidden. They made a dash to seize my rifle as I unslung it from my shoulders, but they were not quick enough. In a second the fourth fellow—the one sitting down—had jumped up to help his companions.

One fellow got somewhat of a dent in his skull with the butt of my rifle, the others, unluckily, ran away, and I did not pursue them, as I needed all the strength I possessed to go up the pass. As the Tibetans disappeared in the direction I had come

I became rather alarmed for my men, lest they should be taken by treachery, but I knew they could take care of themselves.

After taking a rest, for the violent exertion had caused me a deal of panting and blowing, I continued. I soon got out of the *débris* and boulders, where I proceeded with great caution, and got upon the snow on the north side of the glacier. For real majestic beauty the Nui Glacier cannot be surpassed. It has immense terraces of clear greenish ice, quite regular and well padded with snow on the surface; gigantic crevasses, down which one was almost afraid to look, and a background of huge white sharp-edged peaks, like the teeth of a saw, so white indeed that the stormy sky beyond looked as black as ink. It was truly one of the most impressive scenes I have ever set eyes upon. I never feel very big on any occasion, but I do not remember ever feeling quite so small and humble and insignificant as I did on that particular occasion—a mere speck, a mere black spot, disturbing the peaceful harmony of the grandiose landscape.

I have attempted to depict the scene in one of the illustrations, but no brush nor canvas can satisfactorily reproduce the immensity of those white mountains towering around you, the in-

THE NUI GLACIER

calculable masses of snow, the almost terrifying appearance of the immense cracks in the ice hundreds of feet deep. It gave you a certain feeling of loneliness and helplessness in case of mishap, and it really made you think a good deal of how small are human beings and how puerile all their works, when compared to those accomplished by the hand of Nature.

I think it would be a good thing if a great many other authors—not to speak of our critics, who need it even more—could have an opportunity of experiencing the sensation of humility I had upon me that day.

But, humble or not, I went on and on, like a tiny little ant upon the immaculate and endless white carpet of snow, and higher and higher I gradually rose upon the mountain side towards the Nui Pass. Panting and blowing, and with a feeling that I wanted to throw away the rifle and cartridges and cameras and instruments that I was lugging up with me—oh, they were such a weight! always in the way, and ever dangling where you did not want them,—I got higher along a narrow furrow so steep as to be almost vertical. I went up for a time on loose rocks which gave way under me, and were most trying to the temper. One could not help constant falling, and one's poor fingers and toes got jammed to a pitiable extent.

Overhead a storm was brewing which promised to be of the very worst kind; but luckily in the last portion of the ascent I was screened somewhat from the cutting wind. Getting up to the top was a terrible effort, carrying all my paraphernalia, but at last, in a desperate struggle, I managed to get there.

The Nui Pass itself, as can be seen by the drawing I give in these pages, is a very narrow opening, in parts quite free from snow owing to its steepness and to being so boxed in. Besides, on the south side, by which I ascended, it is rather more covered, because the snow is generally driven with much fury from the north. In fact, when I reached the summit and proceeded for some distance on the Tibetan side (north aspect), the mountain was thickly padded with uninterrupted snow. The wind was so fierce up there that it knocked me clean off my feet twice.

Now came the tedious job of boiling water in the hypsometrical apparatus to ascertain the altitude, and taking whatever photographs and sketches I found possible. But I had no sooner begun to unpack my instruments in a sheltered

ASCENT TO THE NUI PASS.

nook than the storm broke out in all its violence, and the snow, driven with tremendous force by the wind into my face, felt just like hundreds of needles and nails thrown at me. I wasted two entire boxes of matches in setting the hypsometrical stove alight, and to accomplish this I had to protect it with my coat, of which I had divested myself. I have never envied the Chinese gods with a hundred arms more than I did on this occasion, for one's two hands were required in twenty places at the same time, the wind blowing everything about in a most reckless manner. The water seemed to take ages to boil, and the storm was getting worse and worse every moment, almost freezing my poor hands, nose and ears, and giving me intense pain.

At last the welcome puff of steam began to escape from the apparatus; the temperature of boiling water (178°·1) and the temperature of the air (30°) were duly registered, and I repacked everything to make my descent. The altitude—the correct one—of this pass in feet by hypsometrical apparatus was 19,621 feet, and two excellent aneroids I also carried registered 19,600 feet.

A great deal is to be said for and against

aneroids. In a few words, this is my experience of them as regards work at great elevations. Unless you can get aneroids of tested excellence and the very best that money can procure, you had better go without them. Very small aneroids may be more portable, but they are never of any real use. Always carry your aneroids yourself, and never let them go out of your sight if you want to keep them in good order, and never rely on them too much except when constantly checked by boiling-point thermometers. Personally, for important elevations, I have relied entirely on boiling-point thermometers, the only practical and less cumbersome way of accurately ascertaining heights for an explorer, but I also always carry several aneroids, two specially constructed for me to measure down to 12 inches—over 25,000 feet—and I have invariably found them accurate. I use them only for differential altitudes, and for the less important observations.

CHAPTER XIX

AND now for the descent. I was quite numbed with cold—you see, a thin shirt only is not much protection against snow being driven into you with such force, and even when I put on my coat again my teeth were chattering so that I thought they would break. Well, I suppose that if I had been more muffled up and wearing heavy clothing I should have never got up there. My legs and hands had nearly lost all feeling in them.

I loaded my rifle and all my instruments on my back, also my straw hat which it was impossible to wear in the right place, bade Tibet a hearty "good-bye," and down I strode, with somewhat disjointed steps, by the way I had come. The descent was rapid—a great deal too rapid—but partly to get away from the intense cold, and the wind and the snow, partly owing to the anxiety which I still felt regarding the safety of my two men I had left behind,

I really did not try to control my speed. When I got among the loose rocks again, which started a regular landslide at each step one took, I came very near having an accident which might have had disastrous consequences. A stone rolled under my foot—they nearly all did—and in slipping I got my right foot badly jammed between two large stones. Before I had time to get it off again, several big stones came rolling with great force from above, and one hit me so violently in the leg, and on falling upon the other rocks squeezed my ankle with such pressure that I really thought my leg had been fractured. Fortunately it was not.

The pain was excruciating, my feet being still half-frozen, and I sat down, rubbing the one foot to restore some life to it, but it swelled considerably and hung like dead, which caused me some little apprehension. Violent friction with snow I tried next, and this seemed to bring some warmth and circulation, but the pain was intense. One fact was certain, that it was getting late in the afternoon, and that the Nui Pass was not the kind of place where I should care to be benighted, so down I struggled, limping badly, and suffering agony every time the foot got jammed again, which was at an average about every minute.

OBSERVATIONS FOR ALTITUDE TAKEN UNDER DIFFICULTIES ON THE NUI PASS, DARMA

Thank heavens! I then got to the snow incline, where I could practise some tobogganing, which saved much time and labour, and down I slid, carefully regulating my speed upon the snow with my good leg. You see, if one had gone too fast one might have been shot into one of the big crevasses of the Nui Glacier down below, and that I particularly wished to avoid.

Partly through the strain of carrying up such a heavy load, partly through the very little sleep I had obtained of late, partly owing to the great glare of the immense white mountains before me during the day, and also in a measure to the biting wind and snow—not to speak of the pain I was undergoing—the vision of the only good eye I possessed became affected and caused me additional trouble. At moments my sight became obscured altogether.

There is no doubt that it is well worth going up any high mountain for the sake of the relief and satisfaction one experiences on coming down again, and on no occasion did I feel this more strongly than upon that day. When I got down to the glacier again—which spreads from east to west—I felt much better, and although still quite lame could proceed at a fair pace.

I hastened down to rejoin my two men, for the evening was drawing in. I took special care not to fall into another snare—as surely the Tibetans might attempt some of their games again—but nothing happened. Nothing ever does when you are on your guard.

It was getting dark when I arrived at the spot where my two followers had remained, and I shouted myself hoarse, but got no reply. I looked for them in several places where they might possibly be, but I could find no signs of them. Again I shouted and shouted, but no reply. Had they been murdered or had they gone away? This was particularly tantalising, because not only did I feel for their loss, but I also wanted badly to get rid of the load I was carrying.

By a mere chance, possibly suggested by my close observation of Shoka ways, I thought that, before departing to rejoin the main portion of my expedition, I would inspect some huge boulders some way off, behind which the men in their long hours of waiting might possibly have taken shelter. Had they been there, with the howling wind they could not possibly hear my voice. In fact, under the largest boulder, where the melting snow had formed a hollow, I discovered my two Shokas wrapped up, head and all, in their blankets, and snoring hard. They had given me up for lost—although the idea did not disturb their sleep—and were waiting till the next morning to proceed up the glacier to look for me.

The four Tibetans had tried to approach them, pretending friendship, but they wisely had driven them away with stones. Then, for safety, they had at sunset removed their quarters to a more secluded spot. The distance from this spot to the Nui Pass and back was six miles.

The storm was still very bad, snow was again falling plentifully, and we decided that our best plan was to make a night march—long as it would be—and try to rejoin the others. Relieved of the weight of rifles and all, I was able to get along pretty well, except that after we had gone a couple of miles it got pitch dark, and we stumbled against everything and got terribly jerked. It snowed hard, and the wind blew in all its fury. We eventually came upon the faint trail, now white with snow, but on this it was considerably easier to proceed. We travelled now on long stretches of flat country, then upon an undulating, even hilly, portion of the valley, occasionally resting for breath under the lee of some big rock, and drawing freely on my supply of chocolate, which one of my men carried.

Towards midnight we reached an open space—one of the camping-grounds—called Bedang, where the Tibetans have erected three extensive *mani* or sacred walls, one with a number of images. We got on the lee side of it, and, taking bundles of matches, lighted them up to inspect the long row of coloured Buddhas forming a cornice to the upper part of the wall. There were dozens of these images, evidently all made in the same mould, and painted in combinations of yellow, red, and blue. Then there were large stones with the usual sacred inscription, and flying prayers wherever they could be hung.

Half-way between Bedang and the Nui camping-ground we had come across a number of *chirams* (pyramids, often tombs) and *chokdens.*

By the time we had reached this sacred spot we were pretty well tired out and hungry, but we had not sufficient blankets to go round nor food enough to make us feel really happy again. We rested a while, and before our limbs got numbed with cold we again started off on our dreary march to rejoin the main body of my party. As we got lower down we came in for a violent shower of hail—the

WE CAME UPON A SHRINE OF CURIOUS BUDDHA IMAGES

pellets being of such a size that they thumped rather too vigorously on our skulls—then torrents of rain. We were simply soaked. It cleared for a few moments, and the moon shone for some seconds between two ugly black clouds—almost, it seemed, only to laugh at us. Indeed, a moment later another downpour froze us to the marrow of our bones, and it was all we could do to proceed at all.

There was, fortunately, a narrow trail here, which we followed, and which frequently overhung precipices of great height. In several places the trail was actually resting on crowbars thrust into the face of the cliff. We stumbled along, but we were all so tired out that we really cared little what happened to us. The hours seemed interminable.

At 3.30 A.M. we at last approached Go village. All the houses were shut up, everything was as still as death, until we got quite close. Then dogs barked furiously from every house, and the noise was echoed from mountain to mountain. The weather had somewhat cleared, but nowhere could I discern my tents. We shouted and yelled to rouse the head village man, and eventually the scared figure of a Shoka appeared, lighted by a red blaze from a torch he carried in his hand. He was jovial, and most anxious to be of assistance.

Although not absolutely, I am, practically, a teetotaller, as I seldom require stimulants, but on that particular occasion I would have given all the money I possessed to have a glass—or, better, a bottle—of stout! But, alas! the nearest bottle of stout was a great many days' journey from there. *Chökti*, the native liquor, was the only stuff procurable, and I more than jumped at the offer when the chieftain suggested that we must drink some to be revived.

Now, there is nothing a Shoka admires more in a foreigner than appreciation of the national *chökti* —an appreciation they seldom get, for *chökti* is, indeed, the vilest concoction a human mind can conceive or a human throat swallow.

When the Shoka and his torch disappeared we listened from the door with ever-increasing attention to noises of dangling keys being tried, one after the other, into a lock. Then came the snapping sound of the opening padlock, next the loosing of the iron chain which is ever used in bolting Shoka doors. Reproachful noises from the household, interrupted in their sleep, and remonstrative cries of female relatives, could be heard at intervals;

then a long silence, some rattling about, and at last the chieftain reappeared, triumphantly nursing a huge jug of the "reviver."

"Will you drink it here or down in your tent?" he inquired, with a twinkle in his eye.

"In the tent," I replied; and we all went down to where my camp had been pitched. My men sprang out from all sides on hearing my voice, especially several of them who, not expecting me back that night, had thought fit to occupy my tent.

In a few moments the camp was alight with several blazing fires, there being plenty of fuel at this place, and from the village a string of figures with torches were running down, bringing food, more fuel, milk, and vegetables. The natives of Go were indeed most thoughtful and polite.

I had marched continuously for twenty-two and a half hours, covering over forty miles, the entire time over most difficult ground and at such great elevation that when I sat down upon my blankets I felt quite exhausted. Nor did devouring—the word eating is hardly expressive enough—several pounds of rice and meat and potatoes and plum-pudding and milk and *chökti* make me feel any better. My appetite was insatiable, and no sooner was my head laid on the pillow than I was fast asleep. Oh, what a lovely sensation to go to sleep when you are so tired!

CHAPTER XX

We were already getting to lower elevations—the village of Go being only 10,577 feet. We had to the west of us the great Nanda Devi, the highest mountain in the British Empire, 25,660 feet; three pyramidal peaks, with rock exposed in vertical streaks right up to the summit. The central peak is Nanda Devi itself, the next highest peak being 24,379 feet, according to Trigonometrical Survey measurements.

There are several extensive glaciers to the east watershed of Nanda Devi, mostly extending from west to east, with a slight tendency northwards, but on the western side of the watershed Nanda Devi is practically surrounded by an immense glacier with numerous ramifications.

There are a great many legends regarding this imposing mountain, the principal one stating that on the shores of a lake which is supposed to exist on the very summit of Nanda is the abode and present residence of Vishnu. The natives state that smoke is often seen rising from the summit, which, they say, is caused by the god's kitchen. Some considerable distance below the summit, as high as one can possibly climb, a festival is held every twelve years, but so difficult is the ascent that many pilgrims perish, and only very few can reach the elevated spot. Those few are held in great respect by their fellow-countrymen.

Nearer us than Nanda Devi and also to our west were two other giants (21,520 feet and 22,660 feet), showing characteristics very similar to Nanda Devi. The former had an immense glacier, the Naulphu, on its eastern side, with huge masses of clear ice of resplendent beauty when the sun shone on them. The ice terraces were fairly regular, much more so than in most other glaciers I had inspected. At the bottom of the glacier, in the centre, was an immense wall of ice, horse-shoe-shaped, a most impressive sight as it stood out in brilliant relief above the dark-brown *débris* of the terminal moraine. The Neo-lak-chan River has its birth from this glacier.

There were three or four picturesque little Shoka hamlets along the river—especially near the spot where the Lissar River, fed by a number of glaciers to the north-west, meets the Dholi River, which we have followed from the Nui Glacier to the north. The village of Dukti was quite attractive, with houses painted white, slate roofs, and strongly built store-houses.

The trail mostly followed the course of the Dholi River, and was often boxed in between high vertical cliffs of grey rock, along which the road was constructed on crowbars. Between the villages of Bahling (10,230 feet) and Nagling (9876 feet—h.a.) was another small but interesting glacier of dirty grey ice mixed with mud and *débris*, and a central and two side dunes. A stream rose from it and became a tributary of the Dholi.

From Nagling to Shobla there is a fair road, and from Sela, about half-way between the two above villages, it is possible to get over the mountains to Kuti. The way, however, is extremely bad, and over a good deal of snow. The journey occupies from three to four days.

From Nagling southward the road was almost an identical replica of the Nerpani—the waterless trail—I had followed on the way out. In many places it was supported on crowbars and we had a drop under us of several hundred feet.

As far as Go from Nui the trail was on the east side of the Dholi River; from Go it was on the west side. Some two miles from Shobla one got a charming bird's-eye view of this village, with the river like a ribbon of silver winding its way between high mountains covered with luxuriant vegetation. Perhaps the beautiful deep green of the trees affected us all the more because we had been so long among barren, desolate, dreary landscapes, and among snow and ice; so that it was a regular feast for our eyes to see some signs of vegetation again.

The Darma Shokas, like those of Bias, only inhabit these villages during the summer months, retiring to warmer regions farther south (mainly to Dharchula) for the winter. Hence, a great many temporary sheds can be seen in all their villages, wherein are stored their articles of furniture, mats, and clothing, which they do not require when busy trading in the summer months. In some spots the mountain side was simply dotted with these temporary store-houses.

As we were going towards Khela, where we should complete the circle of our journey and meet another contingent of my men who had proceeded there direct from Nepal, we had no further adventures worth mentioning, except one.

We came to a strange cave, only a few yards deep and some 30 feet high, in the side of a hill. The natives had told me that no animal could enter it without dying, and, in fact, when we peeped into it we saw a number of skeletons of dogs, other small mammals, and birds. On stooping down, one of my men and I were immediately seized with giddiness and a fainting sensation, and had we not been quick enough in jumping out into the open air we might have possibly collapsed, owing to the noxious gases which emanated from the ground in the cave. A peculiar sulphurous odour was noticeable, even some little distance from the cave. It is in its effects very much like the "Grotta dei Cani" of Naples, only this one seemed more deadly. The gases seem to hang low upon the ground, not more than about 3 or 3½ feet, although on entering the cave one felt at once a stifling sensation, even when standing upright. We two who had stooped suffered from a severe headache for some hours.

Before we leave the Darma district, a word on the history of the natives may be of interest. The Darma Shokas are in many ways—and in facial appearance—very different from the Shokas of Chaudas and Bias, and, although their origin is undoubtedly Mongolian from Tibet, their traditions vary very considerably from those of the other Shokas. According to some authorities the Darma Shokas are the descendants of a horde of Mughals who were endeavouring to take possession of Kumaon during the time that Timur was occupying a portion of that country. This horde, which is supposed to have entered Kumaon from the plains and not over the mountains, was eventually reduced to very small numbers, and driven to the mountains, where they finally settled, practically undisturbed, in the Darma Valley. Darma, like the other Shoka districts (Bias and Chaudas), formerly belonged to Tibet, and it was not till the Gorkhali administration that Darma, with Bias and Chaudas, was annexed to Kumaon.

Even now, as we have already seen, the Tibetans exercise a serious influence upon those natives, the Shokas of all these districts, however willing to be faithful and loyal to us, having never received protection nor the meagrest justice from the British Government.

Personally, I do not quite share the opinion that the Darma Shokas came from the plains or from

THE SACRIFICE OF A YAK

At the death of a tribesman the animal is precipitated from a high cliff on which it has been driven.

Tibet by way of the plains. They resemble quite closely the Kam-par or Tibetans from Kam, with whom they are to this day in constant communication. In fact, it is chiefly with the Kam-par tribe and Gyanema that the Darma Shokas do all their trading. The more massive features and stronger facial characteristics of the Darma Shokas have been acquired, I think, more through their frequent intercourses with Jumlis and other tribes of Western Nepal, which gives them a wilder appearance than the more purely Mongolian stolid types, such as the Bias Shokas.

In many ways the Darma Shokas do not possess the refined and gentlemanly feelings so strikingly common among Bias Shokas, nor are they quite so honest and reliable. But they, too, possess good hearts, are somewhat impetuous and excitable, and occasionally addicted to murder.

CHAPTER XXI

From Khela on the Nepalese boundary, where I found my men and pony—the latter had been safely taken back across the dangerous Nerpani road—I proceeded in all haste to Almora. I varied my journey slightly, travelling by way of Thal.

The roar of British officials had been very great while I was distant, so I halted several days both in Almora and Naini-Tal, the summer seat of the Provincial Government, in order to give them opportunity of carrying out some of their threats. Nothing happened.

By way of Bombay I returned to England, and from there I sailed directly to America, on my way to the Chinese War.

Perhaps the journey, requiring as it did more than ordinary endurance, did more to strengthen my former theories about travelling attendants than any journey I had taken before. I invariably

GOATS CARRYING LOADS OF BORAX

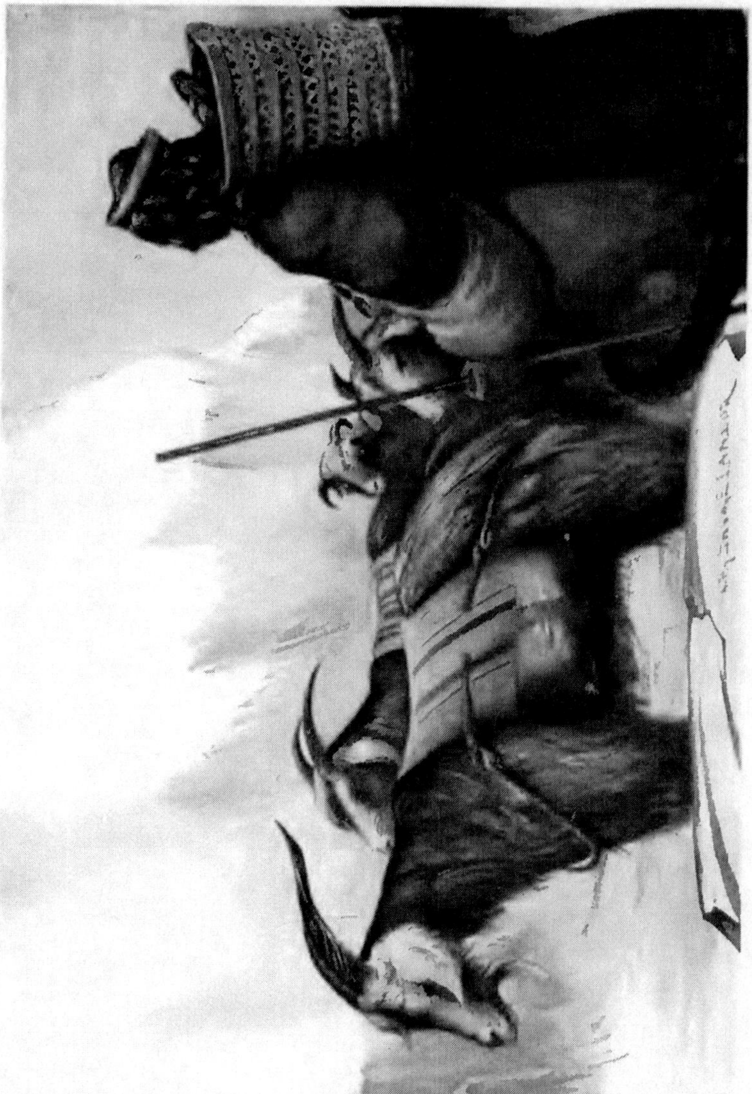

found that thoughtful and tactful kindness with my men and with strangers always paid better than harsh treatment. It is all very well for the leader of an expedition not to mind this, and not to feel that, and, if anything, rather enjoy the fun of roughing it. The interest which he—if of even moderate intelligence—must take in the study of the country, the natives, recording his scientific observations, surveying, photographing, writing up his notes, etc., leave him but little time to worry over climatic conditions or the cooking. But not so with the native followers, who after their day's work is finished—and pretty tedious their day's work is—have nothing to employ their minds except the thought that another day of hardship is to follow. The mind preys a good deal upon the entire system, and when to mental depression you add every possible bodily inconvenience you can think of, it is not unnatural that the men are inclined to break down.

First of all, naturally, I took great care to have my men well fed and clothed, then the next and most important was to prevent them getting depressed when great difficulties were facing them. Many evenings, when we did not make night marches, I used to collect my men round my tent

15

and entertained them with long descriptions of things in Europe they had never seen, such as ocean steamers, "sky-scrapers," railways, electric light, etc.

I am rather sorry that, this publication being illustrated entirely by drawings done by hand, I am not able to give an interesting photograph of a group of my followers whom I snapshotted as I was describing to them the wonders of civilisation. The expressions of wonderment and keen interest were quite intense, and show clearly in the photograph.

The men always looked for these nightly lectures, and no matter how tired they were they generally collected round for me to tell them more. This, I think, helped more to keep my men in good spirits—in very exasperating circumstances—than anything I could think of. Every topic would lead to endless discussions among them, and most amusing controversies, which enlivened their spirits, anyhow till the next lecture.

Natives always take the keenest interest in firearms and anything connected with them. Also in telescopes, which they love. I happened to possess a little camera which was not unlike a spy-glass. I had given it to one of my men to carry—by the

YAKS AND PONIES CONVEYING WOOL
ACROSS THE FRONTIER

A. HENRY SAVAGE LANDOR

way, to the fellow who saved my life on the top of Lumpa Mountain. He could not get it out of his head that it was a glass, and once or twice I caught him trying to survey the landscape with it.

One evening, on my way down to Almora, we had reached camp, and as I was sitting outside my tent I perceived the fellow walking away with my camera towards a cluster of trees some way off on the top of a hillock. I watched him with the corner of my eye. When he got there he climbed right to the top of the highest tree, and as he clung with his folded legs to the branch, swinging to and fro in the wind, he unslung the camera and pulled it out of its case. Next, as I expected, he brought it up to his eyes and proceeded to scan the landscape. Unhappily for the camera, the branch, having swung rather too far beyond its limit of elasticity, gave way, and down came the man and precious instrument, bounding from branch to branch until they bumped with some might upon the solid ground—the man, of course, on the top of the camera. The camera he picked up in fragments, besides destroying eighteen excellent negatives it contained.

"What on earth did you do that for?" I asked of the Shoka.

"*Sahib*," he said, rubbing his aching side, "I have longed for many a day to look through the *durbin*; we Shokas are to leave you to-morrow, and I thought I would have no other opportunity. You can kill me, *sahib*, because I deserve it!"

When I thought of the deep debt of gratitude I owed this man, I preferred to spare him. I handed him a real and powerful telescope, properly focussed, for him to have the treat he wished. When he gazed through it and saw the distant snows and a village some miles off appear quite close, his excitement had no bounds, and when he recognised people coming out of the houses his amazement was very curious to watch.

We had many, many amusing incidents of this kind, and they served to pass away the time.

I cannot end this book without paying a tribute to the faithfulness, endurance, and bravery of all my men. A more devoted lot of fellows could nowhere have been procured. I never had the slightest trouble in any way with them even, as we have seen, under most trying circumstances. The work demanded of them was of the most severe nature, and the constant strain and bodily sufferings so great, that I rather doubt whether I know of any white man who could have stood it—not as they did, but even half as well. As it was, after the strain was over—but not before—the poor fellows all broke down, except one. Most of them were pitiably footsore and exhausted, and only their strong will carried them through. The only exception was the young boy, frail and delicate, almost girlish-looking—but with a determined little face—to whom I have referred at the beginning of the book. As stipulated when I employed him, he always carried the heaviest load, and when physically stronger men lay down tired at the end of a march, he was ever ready to run about to collect fuel, took endless pleasure in helping to pitch the tents, and assist in the cooking. The endurance and courage of that little fellow were quite marvellous. He did more work than two men taken together, and at the end of the journey he was the only one who returned in excellent condition, and as fresh as possible.

So that, remember, it is not always the big, bulky, muscular fellows who can stand more hardships,—the strongest and most muscular fellow I had was the only one who succumbed; on the contrary, down to a certain limit, for very hard work, the smaller the men you employ the better. Wiriness, suppleness, agility—and intelligence—are essential, and always to be preferred to brutal, uncontrollable strength; but, above all, use your judgment, and never take with you on expeditions of this sort a man who does not possess a strong will.

INDEX

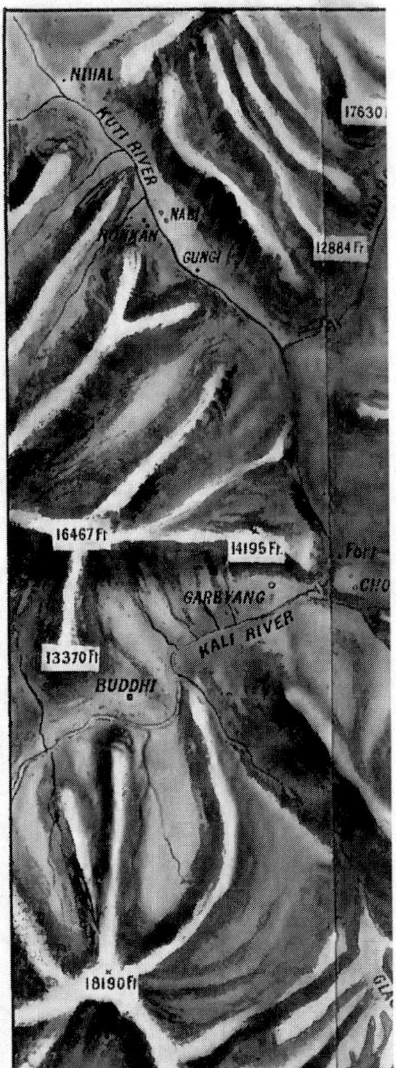
NIHAL
KUTI RIVER
GUNGI
17630
12884 Ft.
16467 Ft
14195 Ft.
Fort
GARBYANG
KALI RIVER
13370 Ft
BUDDHI
18190 Ft

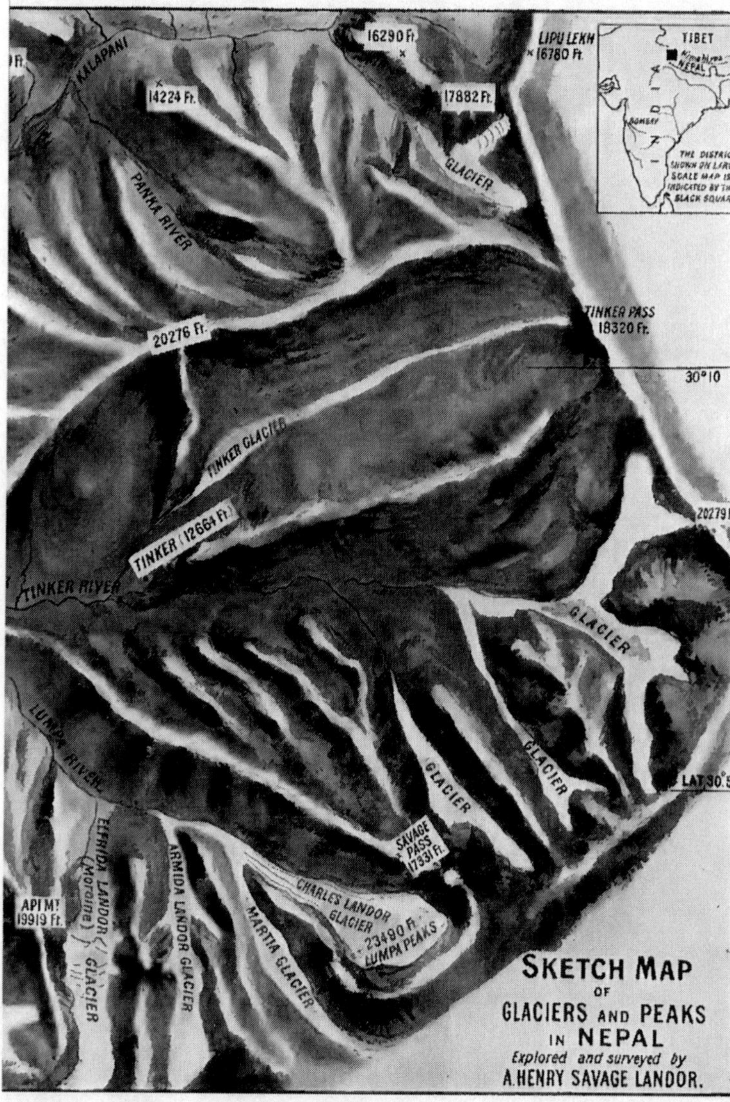
KALAPANI
14224 Ft.
16290 Ft.
17882 Ft.
LIPU LEKH
×16780 Ft.
TIBET
NEPAL
BOMBAY
THE DISTRICT SHOWN ON LARGE SCALE MAP IS INDICATED BY THE BLACK SQUARE
GLACIER
PANKA RIVER
TINKER PASS 18320 Ft.
20276 Ft.
30°10
TINKER GLACIER
TINKER (12664 Ft.)
20279 Ft
TINKER RIVER
GLACIER
LUMPA RIVER
GLACIER
GLACIER
LAT 30°5
SAVAGE PASS 17331 Ft.
ELFRIDA LANDOR (Moraine) GLACIER
ARMIDA LANDOR GLACIER
CHARLES LANDOR GLACIER
23490 Ft. LUMPA PEAKS
MARTIA GLACIER
API MT 19919 Ft.
SKETCH MAP OF GLACIERS AND PEAKS IN NEPAL
Explored and surveyed by
A. HENRY SAVAGE LANDOR.